Xiaomi

Praise for *Xiaomi*

'Jayadevan P.K. takes us on a fascinating journey that covers the rise of Xiaomi—from Beijing to Bengaluru and rest of the world. Xiaomi's phenomenal success is worth studying, especially for challenger brands and start-ups that have a good fight in them. This book is a must-read for anyone aspiring to build a start-up. It unpacks elements of strategy that make modern companies different and successful, even when facing fierce incumbents.'

KUNAL SHAH
CEO & FOUNDER, CRED

'This highly engaging book tells the story of Xiaomi's origin and also unpacks the elements of strategy that made it successful as it scaled up. It is an essential read for everyone who wants to know how modern companies are built on extreme customer centricity.'

GIRISH MATHRUBOOTHAM
CO-FOUNDER & CEO, FRESHWORKS INC.

'Jayadevan P.K. has been tracking technology and start-ups in India for more than a decade. This book on Xiaomi promises to be insightful and an engaging read. There are very few companies that have challenged the status quo, scaled so rapidly and become globally successful.'

AMOD MALVIYA
CO- FOUNDER, UDAAN

'I've been observing Xiaomi's role in globalizing Chinese products since the company's early days. Lei Jun was one of a new generation of entrepreneurs who saw what was possible with the direct-to-consumer model and started to push China forward as an innovator that could show the US a thing or two. This book shines a light on one of the world's most important consumer technology company with hard-to-come-by insights and perspective.'

HAMISH MCKENZIE
CO-FOUNDER OF SUBSTACK; AUTHOR OF
*BETA CHINA: THE DAWN OF AN INNOVATION
GENERATION*

Xiaomi

How a Start-up Disrupted the Market and Created a Cult Following

JAYADEVAN P.K.

**HARPER
BUSINESS**

An Imprint of HarperCollins Publishers

First published in India in 2021 by Harper Business
An imprint of HarperCollins *Publishers*
A-75, Sector 57, Noida, Uttar Pradesh 201301, India
www.harpercollins.co.in

2 4 6 8 10 9 7 5 3 1

P-ISBN: 978-93-9032-704-1
E-ISBN: 978-93-9032-705-8

Typeset in 12/16.2 Adobe Garamond at
Manipal Technologies Limited, Manipal

Printed and bound at
Thomson Press (India) Ltd.

To
Dhruva

Contents

Contents

Author's Note

MANY YEARS AGO, I had joined the local news desk of a prominent newspaper in Bengaluru, the sleepy south Indian town that became the country's Silicon Valley. After trying my hand at crime reporting and general business journalism, I developed an interest in tracking technology. Among other things in the mid noughties, I had half a page in the paper to feature new gadgets every week. Nokia, Blackberry, Samsung and a few other companies were regulars on the page. While I was enjoying my work, my salary needed a boost. (The media industry's decline was just about beginning, and salaries were as poor then as they are today.)

Getting out of the rather difficult circumstances that I found myself in, I moved on to the *Economic Times* to report on technology. The business daily was India's largest pink paper by circulation, and I worked with some of the best journalists of the time. My job was mainly to write about technology services companies. Soon I got bored with tracking quarterly results and rehearsed statements. This was around 2012, and India's start-up ecosystem was in its infancy. I quit the paper to join a start-up blog. I didn't ask for a raise. I was just happy to be able to write about start-ups and their founders. It was something new, and their excitement was infectious. In those days, 'start-up' was not a mainstream beat in India. Only niche blogs wrote about them.

On the personal front, there were months when I was flat broke. One evening I sold my old Nokia 5800 for ₹300 at a second-hand electronics shop to buy a packet of biryani. That is still the best biryani I've ever had. The two years at the start-up blog were also my best two years ever. As start-ups became the buzzword, I went back to the pink paper to write about them. I was able to upgrade my life a little. I moved into a middle-class apartment with my family. I got some furniture and so on. After selling the Nokia phone, I used a feature phone for a few days. But now I had to upgrade my phone. After much research, I zeroed in on a Micromax handset.

Micromax, a Gurgaon-based company that began making handsets in 2008, had some smartphones that were affordable on a young journalist's salary. It was also a leading brand and had some interesting features such as dual SIM and a great touchscreen display. Going from a phone that ran on Symbian (Nokia's proprietary operating system that failed) to an Android-based phone was like suddenly being able to breathe after being underwater for a while. There were tens of thousands of apps to play with and an operating system that worked really well.

But I soon realized that I was running out of memory faster than I could delete apps, music and photos. The phone began to slow down, and I was starting to get that same sinking feeling

I had the evening I sold the Nokia phone. It was beginning to frustrate me. Around the same time, I had the opportunity to visit the office of e-commerce firm Flipkart for a story about how it scaled its back-end systems to meet the unprecedented demand for a new phone. The phone was a relatively unknown brand called Xiaomi. And everybody was surprised it sold out so quickly. In fact, they even thought their website had a glitch when buyers complained that they were getting 'out of stock' messages. But it turned out that, just like me, there were millions of Indians waiting for a credible (and affordable) alternative to the models then available.

The phone was priced unbelievably low for the features it offered, and that was its main draw. This was the sweet spot Xiaomi hit. As the years went by, I watched Xiaomi's phenomenal growth in India. It swept away Micromax and other Indian brands and became India's largest smartphone company.

In the winter of 2018, I went to Beijing on a reporting assignment. I suddenly had the urge to meet Xiaomi's co-founder Lei Jun, whom I'd seen at a press conference earlier in Bengaluru. I wrote an email to the company's communications team but did not get to meet Lei. I did the next best thing: I hung out at Xiaomi's first store in Beijing, near its headquarters in Haidian. I also took a stroll in Haidian Park, where I saw real-world applications of artificial intelligence (AI)—such as a running track that could identify runners and keep score of their mileage, a virtual Shifu who taught tai chi to visitors, and an almost autonomous bus. It was a stunning display of China's technological progress. My previous visit to Beijing was in 2011, and the difference was evident. China's Silicon Valley was evolving rapidly. And in it, companies like Xiaomi were hatching world-domination plans. I was awestruck and a little sad. My admiration was tainted with melancholy because I had seen Bengaluru, India's Silicon Valley, evolve into an urban mess just like most Indian cities that once held promise. At the same time, China seemed to have pulled ahead to become a global superpower. I had begun to track Chinese technology companies and their growth back in India closely. The seeds of this book were sown in my head then. Xiaomi's rise and global success is an amazing story of many factors that came together. Its resounding success in India encouraged many more Chinese companies to look at India as a potential market. Xiaomi's playbook is also a delight to decode. It is as if someone has masterfully knit together a future-proof strategy, carefully picking elements from many different industries and backed it with heads-down execution. It was a happy coincidence that a publisher was also looking for a book on Xiaomi. I got to know of this through a friend, and the book became a serious pursuit last year. I have tried to capture Xiaomi's journey from a little-known software company in Beijing to one of the youngest companies to enter the hallowed Fortune 500 list. I've also interspersed the book with elements of strategy that may be useful for other start-ups to understand. Xiaomi is also not very well understood. Most people still see it as a smartphone company. But Xiaomi's ambitions lay much beyond that. The book attempts to throw light on the company's strategy to become an internet company and how user-centricity is core to it.

I've put together this book after dozens of interviews and many hours of research. The book wouldn't have been possible had it not been for the diligent research and hard work by Anwesha Ghosh and the patience my editor Sachin Sharma of

HarperCollins has shown. Also, thanks to Tanmoy Goswami, who put me in touch with Sachin; Josey Puliyenthuruthel, who advised me; Somnath Dasgupta, who made the book readable; Evelyn Fok, who reviewed the book and Ravish Bhatia, who helped me with my research. I am also thankful to my family, especially my wife Radhika, who cheered for me and put up with my moods though I did little to reciprocate their affection. I hope you like what you read.

1

The Whirlwind and Flying Pigs

WHEN XIAOMI CORPORATION, A Chinese company, became the youngest debutant on the Fortune 500 list in 2019—just nine years after it was born—it sent a clear signal to the rest of the world: Chinese product companies had arrived. It was an unprecedented feat for any smartphone company, let alone an unknown upstart from China with a hard-to-pronounce name to boot. Only a few companies had made it to the list this fast in the past. Facebook, for instance, made it to the Fortune 500 list in nine years. Other iconic companies such as Apple and Google made it to the list in their seventh and eighth years, respectively. But unlike these US-based mega-corporations that grew in the fertile grounds of Silicon Valley, Xiaomi was a distinctly Chinese start-up with global ambitions in the midst of the smartphone mega trend that swept across the world.

'It was an important pioneer. It showed that a home-grown Chinese consumer devices company could make world-beating products and market them as well as any US company could,' said Hamish McKenzie, one of the earliest writers from the West to identify Xiaomi as a breakout company and the harbinger of global ambitions nursed by Chinese entrepreneurs for years.[1]

Xiaomi was founded in April 2010 in Beijing at a time when the smartphone industry the world over was in upheaval. Just about three years previously, Apple Inc. and its iconic founder Steve Jobs had disrupted the industry with the launch of the iPhone. Xiaomi's founding also coincided with the rise of China's global ambitions, which had its foundations on over three decades of reforms since the late seventies.

With these great forces coming together, it was a matter of little coincidence that Xiaomi started at that exact juncture when both China and the object of its business were changing rapidly.

When Xiaomi started out, China was a battlefield of over 400 home-grown brands. And while all these brands shared a common history and collectively revolutionized China's smartphone industry, Xiaomi was one of the very few brands that broke through the clutter and cracked several international markets successfully.

In these ten years, Xiaomi has gone from being a smartphone company to a household name. A company that has fostered an entire ecosystem with investments in over 270 other companies that make a wide range of products and are part of Xiaomi's supply chain. Today, it even sells Xiaomi branded t-shirts, pens, robovacs and drones.

---

1   Hamish McKenzie, *Beta China: Dawn of an Innovation Generation*, San
     Francisco: PandoMedia, 2013.

As of November 2020, Xiaomi is the world's third-largest smartphone brand with over 18,960 employees and sells in more than eighty countries. In the first six months of 2020 (the latest available data), Xiaomi sold goods and services worth over $15.7[2] billion at a profit of $862.1 million.[3] It counts over 343.5 million users as monthly active users of its operating system, a modified Android-based platform called MIUI.

In 2018, it went public on the Hong Kong Stock Exchange (HKSE) and raised a record $4.72 billion. It is the youngest company in the Fortune Global 500 list of 2019. In India, the world's second-largest smartphone market where more than half a billion smartphones are in use, Xiaomi has become the largest-selling smartphone brand, beating rival Samsung and wiping out dozens of Indian companies.

Sow the wind

This is the story of Xiaomi, the little-known company that is changing the rules of the game and is no longer just a smartphone company. But before we get to it, we need to wind the clock back to tell another story, which begins with a small family enterprise in Chicago, not Beijing. This family enterprise was known as Galvin Manufacturing Corporation. Today, it is called Motorola. It began in 1928 as a humble family operation led by Paul Galvin, who made the car radio a commercial success in the US two years later. It did not take long for Motorola to build a reputation for itself in technological innovation. From

2 The '$' (dollar) refers to the US dollar unless otherwise mentioned.
3 Annual results announcement for the year ended 31 December 2019 for Xiaomi Corporation.

manufacturing commercialized car radios to developing walkie-talkies for the US army during World War II, Motorola soon became a reliable name in the market and one of the largest companies in the nation. After Paul Galvin's death, his son Robert took the reins of the company. Cut to the eighties. Motorola was looking to expand the business beyond the US. The company was especially keen on entering Japan, a country known for its technological prowess. Breaching the Japanese market turned out to be particularly challenging. Susan Chira wrote in the *New York Times* in 1986:

> 'The saga of Motorola's attempt to enter the cellular telephone market touches on fundamental issues in the trade dispute between the United States and Japan: whether American companies modify their products enough for the Japanese market, how Japan's Government regulates competition, how newcomers to this market can suffer whether they are Japanese or foreign, and how domestic political pressures can outweigh demands from Japan's trading partners.'[4]

The odds were against the company. But Robert 'Bob' Galvin, then chairman of Motorola, was not ready to give up. Motorola finally pushed through in Japan. But Bob's careful considerations led him to a unique and rather prophetic insight that Japan's superiority would soon be trumped by China. In the early seventies, relations between the US and China began to open up. US President

---

4   https://www.nytimes.com/1986/12/15/business/japanese-barriers-slow-motorola-mobile-phone.html

Richard Nixon visited China in February 1972 and met with Chinese Communist Party Chairman Mao Zedong. It took years, but by 1979 the US and China had complete diplomatic relations. The 1972 Nixon visit was the beginning of the end of a twenty-five-year-long stasis between the two countries, and American companies were now eyeing China as a potential manufacturing hub. Take, for instance, popular shoemaker Nike, which started as a reseller of shoes made by Japan's Onitsuka. 'I never thought I'd see it in my lifetime, a US President in the Forbidden City, touching the Great Wall. I thought of my time in Hong Kong. I'd been so close to China, and yet so far. I thought I'd never have another chance. But now I thought, One day? Maybe?' Phil Knight, the founder of Nike, recalled of the year in his book *Shoe Dog*. The shoe company opened its first Mainland China factory in 1981. Not long after, an opportunity presented itself when Bob Galvin was invited to a state ceremony on a tour of China in 1986. Motorola had won a deal to set up a cellular system in China that year.[5] Legend has it that Galvin, who was seated next to the minister of railroads at the ceremony, initiated a conversation that would change everything—both at Motorola and in China. Galvin was interested in knowing how the Chinese government worked, but more importantly, he wanted the minister to know that, if allowed, his company Motorola could help China, a large nation with hundreds of millions of people living in poverty, become a world-class society.

Years later, in a feature for *Chicago* magazine, veteran journalist and author Ted C. Fishman wrote about Bob's bluster.

5   https://www.motorola.com/us/about/motorola-history-milestones

'... he broke protocol and turned to the minister of the railroads next to him. Was the minister satisfied doing a serviceable job, Bob asked, or would he prefer to help make China a world-class society? Chinese officials eventually agreed to let Motorola set up manufacturing in the country on one condition: that Motorola teach its Chinese employees and suppliers how to make products good enough for global customers.'[6]

Bob Galvin's persistence paid off. But he knew the downside to this arrangement, Fishman noted. If he agreed, the Chinese would not only learn the tricks of the trade, but they could potentially come after Motorola and rival them at their own game in a few years. But China was a big country with a huge market, which meant despite the competition, Motorola could still survive. Galvin took the deal.

And so began the growth of mobile telephony in China. This was the country's proverbial turning point in electronics manufacturing. Motorola not only entered the Chinese market but also trained the Chinese workforce in the best technology that was available at the time. Around the same time, Taiwanese businesses were also set up in China for their cheap labour. The *New York Times* chronicles the relationship between Taiwanese business and former enemy state China through the story of Tony Lin, a factory manager who went to Mainland China for the first time in 1988, in an article titled The Land that Failed to Fail:

---

6   https://www.chicagomag.com/Chicago-Magazine/September-2014/
     What-Happened-to-Motorola/

'What he [Lin] found surprised him: a large and willing workforce, and officials so eager for capital and know-how that they offered the use of a state factory free and a five-year break on taxes. Mr. Lin spent the next decade shuttling to and from southern China, spending months at a time there and returning home only for short breaks to see his wife and children. He built and ran five sneaker factories, including Nike's largest Chinese supplier.'[7]

Lin was part of the diaspora that brought business to China. 'In effect, Taiwan jump-started capitalism in China and plugged it into the global economy,' Philip P. Pan wrote in the *New York Times*. The Chinese, in their turn, passed down this knowledge to a broader pool of suppliers.

Very soon, China's national communications network was running on Motorola's high-end technology. As Fishman later recalled, 'Altogether, Motorola did more than just about any other foreign company to create a market-ready Chinese industrial complex.' Motorola's Chinese deal was designed to help both parties, but Motorola was the first to reap the benefits. Chinese labour was cheap yet efficient, which meant Motorola was now mass-producing its products at a far lower cost at its Chinese plants than it could back home and shipping them en masse to the American market. By 1994, 60 per cent of Americans using wireless phones were Motorola users.[8] The growing mobile handset business catapulted Motorola to the twenty-third

---

7   https://www.nytimes.com/interactive/2018/11/18/world/asia/china-rules.html

8   https://www.bloomberg.com/news/articles/1998-05-03/how-motorola-lost-its-way

position on the Fortune 500 list of 1994 with $22 billion in revenue and $2 billion in profits.[9] The verdict was out; Galvin's gamble had paid off, and for now Motorola was riding the wave of its new-found success.

But even at its peak, Motorola did not remain completely unchallenged, for a Finnish company named Nokia had been growing in its shadow the whole time. If Motorola prided itself on providing NASA with radio transponders that facilitated the broadcast of Neil Armstrong's famous words, 'One small step for man, one giant leap for mankind', to Earth on the 1969 moon mission, Soviet leader Mikhail Gorbachev used Nokia's first handheld mobile phone, the Mobira Cityman 900, which was launched in 1987, to call in a press conference in Moscow that year.[10] It even earned it a nickname, 'Gorba', after the picture of Gorbachev using the Mobira Cityman became news. In short, both Motorola and Nokia were catalysts to some cutting-edge technological innovations and were directly responsible for the spread of telecommunication services worldwide.

Nokia follows Motorola and China gains

While Motorola may have been the largest mobile phone manufacturer in 1994, it was only a matter of time before Nokia overtook it. Nokia had already followed in Motorola's footsteps and entered China around 1985 to set up manufacturing plants and even research and development (R&D) and innovation units.

---

9   https://archive.fortune.com/magazines/fortune/fortune_ archive/1994/04/18/79195/index.htm

10   https://www.techradar.com/in/news/8-nokia-phones-that-changed-the-world

In 1992, the company launched its first commercial phone, the Nokia 1011, and by the mid nineties, it was already struggling to keep up with market demand. If Motorola had not cared about Nokia's success earlier, it definitely did now. Nokia had been establishing local connections since the time it entered China, but in 1998, it made it official. That year, Nokia strategically formed a partnership with China Postel, China's largest mobile phone distributor at the time. As if like clockwork, that very year, Nokia recorded sales of close to 41 million mobile phones and overtook Motorola to become the world's number one in mobile phone sales.[11]

The nineties was an exciting decade for Nokia and Motorola as they tried relentlessly to outsmart one another on their newly acquired Chinese turf to be the number one player. But if there truly was a winner, it was China. For over ten years, the Chinese had watched from the sidelines as these two companies experimented with techniques and strategies to come up with high-end technological innovations. It was just a matter of time before local Chinese companies would start using that knowledge to produce their mobile phone models and meet the rising demands of a booming Chinese populace. Both Nokia and Motorola had unwittingly set themselves up to be disrupted.

Late management guru Clayton Christensen calls this the 'Greek tragedy of outsourcing'.[12] Using the example of American personal computer (PC) maker Dell and Taiwanese company Asus, Christensen convincingly argues in his thesis that

---

11 https://www.gsmarena.com/the_rise_dominance_and_epic_fall__a_brief_look_at_nokias_history-blog-13460.php

12 Clayton Christensen, Karen Dillon, and James Allworth, *How Will You Measure Your Life?* London: HarperCollins Publishers, 2012.

companies should 'never outsource their future'.[13] The argument goes something like this: In the nineties, Dell sold personal computers to Americans like hot cakes. It started with selling cheaper personal computers and gradually moved up the value chain. Soon, Dell became the darling of Wall Street by wringing out more profit from its assets. The next bit, widely considered good business practice, would finally become Dell's Achilles' heel. To improve its profit margins, Dell started outsourcing component-making—first, the easier circuits and then more complex circuits including motherboards—to Asus. Initially, this made sense to financial analysts and Dell executives. The practice enabled Dell to sell more personal computers and spend less on making them. It got to a point where Dell outsourced everything to Asus and kept the brand. But in 2005, Asus started its line of personal computers. 'In this Greek-tragedy tale, Asus had taken everything it had learned from Dell and applied it for itself.'[14] History has witnessed companies rise and fall over this tragic complex. Motorola and a whole lot of other companies would learn their lesson only years later when it was too late to do anything about it. That tragedy wrote itself.

As it happens, both Nokia and Motorola had been using China as a cheap labour source to lower their overall production costs. Fundamentally, these Western companies had a market in China, but no products for China. This arrangement worked out perfectly so long as China had negligible demands. The country's back-breaking work culture and minimum wage rates may have facilitated cheap production, but it also implied that a

---

13 Ibid.
14 https://www.linkedin.com/pulse/greek-tragedy-outsourcing-simon-chan/

large section of the country's working population still considered mobile phones a luxury item and could not afford them. China had only 85 million mobile phone users in 2000, which made up barely 10 per cent of the country's population, according to data from Statista.[15] Therefore, these companies' target consumer base was still out in Europe and the US in the beginning. But as China gradually began to reform its economic policies, it raised minimum wages and improved working conditions. Most importantly, it elevated the living standards of the average Chinese, thereby organically creating demand for high-end 'luxury' products that until then had only been part of the great Chinese fantasy. Author Shaun Rein published *The End of Cheap China: Economic and Cultural Trends That Will Disrupt the World* to help readers understand what reformation in China's labour laws and sudden wage hikes might mean for the global manufacturing industry. Rein, the founder of China Market Research Group, reflected that the end of cheap China might have been bad news for all those foreign companies who depended on it to realize higher profit margins, but it also opened a huge untapped market comprising millions of new Chinese consumers. Indeed, by 2011, China had become the world's largest consumer of luxury items, buying goods worth $15.6 billion.[16] Given the drastic change in circumstances, Nokia and Motorola's inability to tap into the Chinese domestic market would cost them dearly.

And it did. The mid noughties saw China move from being chiefly a producer to becoming both producer and consumer.

---

15 https://www.statista.com/statistics/667798/number-of-mobile-cellular-subscriptions-in-china/

16 Shaun Rein, *The End of Cheap China: Economic and Cultural Trends That Will Disrupt the World*. New Jersey: Wiley Publications, 2012.

Between 2000 to 2010, China's economy grew fivefold from $1.21 trillion to $6.09 trillion. The middle kingdom was well on its way in the latter half of the noughties to becoming the world's second-largest economy and had rapidly lifted over 300 million people out of poverty into the middle class. As domestic demand for mobile phones grew exponentially, companies such as Nokia and Motorola found it increasingly difficult to send products to remote rural areas. The sudden spurt in demand had been a pleasant surprise but one that none of these companies was prepared to meet. The phones that were being manufactured were not customized for Chinese users (such as language settings, wallpaper, or even lunar calendars), and Chinese consumers craved for alternatives. With the growth in China's consumer market, mega businesses such as Alibaba and Tencent also fuelled the economy. The sky-high sales numbers Alibaba celebrates every year on Singles Day (the Chinese Black Friday) is telling of the spike in demand for consumer goods in China. Alibaba sold goods worth $75 billion during the Single's Day sales blitz of November 2020. That is more than 2.5 times the value of goods sold in all of 2020 in India.[17,18]

Reap the whirlwind

A series of missteps had rendered Motorola a shadow of itself. The company brought in former Sun Microsystem executive Ed Zander to revive the company. The Moto Razr launched in 2004 was a big hit. But the company's inability to produce phones that

17   https://edition.cnn.com/2020/11/10/tech/singles-day-2020-alibaba-intl-hnk/index.html

18   https://techcrunch.com/2019/11/11/alibaba-singles-day-record/

catered to the China market led to the loss of market share to rivals such as Samsung.

Zander also decided to collaborate with Apple and put the already popular iPod shuffle in Motorola handsets,[19] and the Moto Rockr was born. Zander had thought it would give his company a 'cool' image. The positioning and marketing campaigns did not resonate with the youth in China. Moreover, just like Bob Galvin previously agreed to teach the Chinese how to make high-quality phones, Zander's partnership with Apple taught the Cupertino computer maker how to make a phone. As Ted Fishman astutely observed, '... much as it had taught the Chinese to compete with it years before, Motorola was teaching one of the most creative, competitive, and consumer-savvy companies of all time how to make a phone'.[20] Two years later, in June 2007, Apple launched its first iPhone.

Speaking at the iPhone's first media launch, Apple's iconic founder Steve Jobs announced amidst loud cheers,

'Every once in a while, a revolutionary product comes along that changes everything ... Today, we are introducing three revolutionary products of this class. The first one is a widescreen iPod with touch controls, the second is a revolutionary mobile phone, and the third is a breakthrough internet communications device ... These are not three separate devices, this is one device ... and we

---

19 https://www.wired.com/2008/01/ff-iphone/

20 https://www.chicagomag.com/Chicago-Magazine/September-2014/ What-Happened-to-Motorola/

are calling it iPhone. Today, Apple is going to reinvent the phone. Here it is.'[21]

According to *USA Today's* estimates, about 700,000 iPhones were sold in the first weekend itself, making it the highest-selling Apple product in history, overtaking the iconic iPod Nano. Needless to say, the mobile phone industry was never quite the same again.

From the eighties to the late nineties, Motorola sold the highest number of mobile phones. Soon, it was Nokia's turn to take the top slot. Between 1998 and 2012, Nokia was the market leader until Samsung toppled Nokia in terms of the number of units sold. In the previous decade, Motorola, Nokia and pioneers of the industry such as Research in Motion (the makers of BlackBerry) lost market share rapidly and became irrelevant to the average smartphone buyer. The gap was filled by Apple, Samsung and several smaller firms. As of the third quarter of 2020, a total of 353.6 million smartphones were shipped worldwide, according to data from International Data Corporation (IDC). Samsung, with a market share of 22.7 per cent, was at the top spot, followed by Huawei at 14.7 per cent, Xiaomi at 13.1 per cent, Apple at 11.8 per cent and Vivo at 8.9 per cent. Three out of five top sellers are now Chinese companies that didn't have any presence in the smartphone market just a decade ago.

Seeing Apple's massive success with the iPhone, Silicon Valley's search engine giant Google realized that becoming a mobile-first company was imperative for its continued success. While the company rallied engineers to rewrite all its services to be mobile-first, it also put its weight behind Android, a mobile phone

---

21 https://www.section.io/engineering-education/the-first-iphone/

operating system that it had acquired in 2005 for an estimated $50 million.[22] By 2008, the first commercial Android-based smartphones were out in the market. This too revolutionized the mobile phone industry in ways that neither Wall Street nor top executives at incumbent handset manufacturing companies such as Motorola or Nokia had imagined.

Both Nokia and Motorola were primarily successful hardware companies that did well in the era of mobile telephony. But they struggled when it came to software and did not navigate the mobile web well. While they successfully put in cameras with more memory and better radio, they did not have a stable operating system with millions of apps. When iOS and Android came along, these companies defiantly pursued their own operating systems. Unfortunately, most of those experiments failed, and the world had moved on. You either had an iOS phone or an Android phone.

As Motorola ceded the number one position to Nokia in the handsets business, its profits took a hit. In the telecom equipment business, Motorola lost ground to home-grown Huawei, which Motorola had almost acquired for $7.5 billion in 2003.[23] Huawei went on to become China's largest privately held company with over $100 billion in revenues, and Motorola's fortunes dwindled. The company laid off 3,500 employees or 5 per cent of its workforce in January 2007.[24] But, that was not enough to arrest the decline. In the first quarter of 2007, the company posted a loss of $366 million, and in May 2007, Motorola said

22 https://en.wikipedia.org/wiki/Android_(operating_system)

23 https://www.ft.com/content/fa8e7ab4-3905-11e9-b856-5404d3811663

24 https://www.infoworld.com/article/2662378/motorola-lays-off-4-000-in-search-for-missing-profit.html

it would lay off 4,000 more employees to cut costs further. After the US government foiled Huawei's bid to acquire Motorola's infrastructure business, it was sold to Nokia–Siemens for $1.2 billion in 2010.[25] After selling the telecom network business to Nokia–Siemens, the consumer-facing business of Motorola (called Motorola Mobility) was sold to Google for $12.5 billion in August 2011.[26] Google mainly acquired the company for its patents. However, in 2014, Google sold Motorola Mobility to Chinese consumer electronics giant Lenovo for $2.91 billion.[27] Lenovo now manufactures and sells smartphones and several other consumer electronics devices under the Motorola brand.

Nokia too had to let go of 1,700 employees worldwide by 2009 after its profits sank by 30 per cent in the third quarter of 2008 and sales fell by 3.1 per cent.[28] In a confessional post addressed to Nokia's employees, CEO Stephen Elop likened Nokia to a burning platform, implying that the end was near. He wrote,

> 'Chinese OEMs are cranking out a device much faster than, as one Nokia employee said only partially in jest, "the time that it takes us to polish a PowerPoint presentation". They are fast, they are cheap, and they

---

25 https://www.nytimes.com/2010/07/20/technology/20nokia.html

26 https://techcrunch.com/2011/08/15/breaking-google-buys-motorola-for-12-5-billion/

27 https://www.washingtonpost.com/business/technology/google-sells-motorola-mobility-to-lenovo-for-291-billion/2014/01/29/92836bce-8932-11e3-833c-33098f9e5267_story.html

28 https://www.thestar.com/business/2009/03/18/nokia_to_issue_1700_layoffs_amid_global_market_swoon.html

are challenging us ... The battle of devices has now become a war of ecosystems, where ecosystems include not only the hardware and software of the device but developers, applications, e-commerce, advertising, search, social applications, location-based services, unified communications, and many other things.'[29]

Elop was right. China was a fast-emerging market with new phone brands popping up every day. In fact, China came to dominate the scene with such zeal and promptitude that by 2012 it had overtaken America as the world's largest smartphone market. As experts later observed, the phenomenon of Chinese consumerism was quite unique. *Fortune* magazine, for instance, explained how 'low-priced, high-tech mobile phones have become objects of desire for many of the 1.36 billion people in China, even though income per capita—after adjusting for purchasing power—is less than a fourth that of the US'.[30] Before long, Chinese companies came to occupy the largest share in their home-grown market. In September 2013, Nokia sold its mobile phone division to Microsoft. In 2016, Finnish company HMD Global Oy acquired Nokia's phone division from Microsoft along with the rights to sell phones under the Nokia brand. Nokia itself operates a telecommunications equipment business under Nokia Networks and a consumer products division under Nokia Technologies.

The smartphone revolution created a vacuum in the Chinese markets. Both Nokia and Motorola, which had dominated China's phone industry for decades, now faced challenges they

29 https://www.wired.com/2011/02/nokia-burning-platform/
30 https://fortune.com/longform/china-smartphone-domination/

could not possibly meet. Apple too did not launch its iPhone in China until October 2009. Meanwhile, China, since the early noughties, had become home to the fastest-growing middle-class population in the world. This had significant implications—as more and more Chinese earned disposable incomes, demand for consumer goods shot up, and the void in the smartphone market had to be urgently filled up.

This marked another turning point in China. Almost overnight, enterprising local phone makers flooded the market with locally produced cheap devices to meet the rising demand. These devices, often made at a 'shanzhai factory', were inexpensive and satisfied the immediate needs. Shanzhai refers to counterfeit goods made in China, and shanzhai factories are characterized by low production values. According to one estimate, in 2007, China produced over 150 million shanzhai phones.[31] But as digital anthropologist Payal Arora notes in her book *The Next Billion Users: Digital Life Beyond the West*, the next billion users wanted their products to be 'fabulous'. Not some cheap knock-off.

It was Google's launch of Android in 2008 that changed the game irrevocably. Android was a customizable mobile operating system, one that was far cheaper than Apple's iOS. It enabled Chinese companies to seriously start contemplating their own brand image. As if to facilitate that vision, that very year, MediaTek, a Taiwanese semiconductor company and microchip supplier, provided a complete reference design for phone chipsets, allowing Chinese manufacturers to produce phones at

---

31 http://en.ce.cn/Industries/Telecoms/200807/19/t20080719_16212016.
    shtml

an unbelievable pace.[32] The integrated chip came with support for Bluetooth, touchscreen, texting, cameras and so on. The little chip from MediaTek spelt doom for old-time legends like Nokia and Motorola as thousands of shanzhai factories, unburdened by the cost of R&D and design, could now produce millions of phones of all shapes and sizes, typically at one-fifth of the price of a licensed phone. Design houses that mushroomed in Shenzhen would create a variety of mainboards, and factories could just buy those to manufacture phones of different form factors, cheaper and faster. A 2011 paper by scholars Zhimin Liao and Xiaofang Chen published in *The Journal of Law & Economics* captures this shift in detail.[33] In 1998, China imposed rather stringent entry regulations on mobile phone manufacturing, ostensibly to protect domestic manufacturers. It issued licences to state-owned enterprises (SoEs), encouraging rent-seeking behaviour. Foreign companies such as Motorola and Nokia were forced to partner with SoEs that had usurped licences and charged hefty sums from their foreign partners. The 2011 paper notes,

'The cost of mobile phones was very substantial until the end of 2003 when the invention of an integrated chip in Taiwan significantly reduced production costs. The integrated chip lowered the threshold for entry into mobile phone production to the point where regulators found it too costly to prevent the mushrooming of illegal firms. Numerous non licensed factories began to produce mobile phones, and cheap illegal mobile phones rapidly flooded the market. The intense competition from these

32 https://mobile.reuters.com/article/amp/idINIndia-29509020070913
33 https://www.jstor.org/stable/10.1086/662991?read-now=1&seq=1

illegal phones caused all licensed manufacturers to suffer large losses in 2004 ... in the following years, most licensed manufacturers were driven to bankruptcy.'

Rents disappeared and the cost of enforcing the licence regime became too big and, ultimately, China relaxed the norms.

But just before Chinese companies seized their domestic market and right after Nokia and Motorola had exited the game, if there was one foreign company that was playing its cards right, it was the South Korean electronics giant, Samsung. Back in the late nineties, when most foreign multinationals treated China as a cheap production base, Samsung had had the foresight to start selling devices to China. Over time, Samsung officials forged a network of distribution outlets and telecom carriers and built a strong retail presence in the country. When Apple finally came calling in China, Samsung had already had such a good run that it was impossible to overtake it. In 2013, Reuters reported, 'Apple works through the same channels, but its relatively late entry means it had a significantly smaller presence. Samsung, for example, has more than 200 official distributors and resellers in Guangzhou province, while Apple lists 95.'[34] Samsung's hard work paid off when in 2013 it emerged as the number one smartphone brand in China.

Despite doing so well against the competition, Samsung's success was, however, short-lived in China. It has taken non-Chinese companies years to understand the quirks of the Chinese consumer. Michael Clendenin, managing director of technology consultancy at RedTech Advisors, had once aptly

---

34 https://www.reuters.com/article/samsung-apple-china/insight-how-
    samsung-is-beating-apple-in-china-idINDEE96P03020130726

observed, 'The Chinese just love features. They want to have 50 different things that they're never going to use.'[35] This failure to constantly churn out new features to meet local demands ultimately became Samsung's stumbling block. It was also the opportunity that companies such as Xiaomi identified and serviced quickly. Samsung had to bow out of the race and quickly went from being the best brand in the market to an 'also ran'. Of course, there were other factors that fuelled the South Korean giant's downfall. The *South China Morning Post* reported,

'The battery fire risk that plagued Samsung's Note 7 in 2016 was a turning point for its fortunes in China, deeply damaging the company's reputation. Then came the double whammy of the political fallout over Seoul's support for a US anti-missile defence system, which saw Beijing encourage the boycotting of Korean products.'[36]

Whether it was Nokia and Motorola's failure to upgrade quickly, or the case of the exploding Samsungs, or standard delays in Apple's product launches, eventually, all these brands had to concede ground in one way or the other to upcoming Chinese competitors.

Truly, over three decades, China's growth was akin to the hockey stick graph; it went from being a sweatshop for foreign phone companies to manufacturing its own products so that, over time, it came to dominate its domestic market. In 2011, market researcher Canalys reported only two of the top ten smartphone

---

35 Ibid.

36 https://www.scmp.com/tech/social-gadgets/article/2134770/how-samsung-went-no-1-also-ran-chinas-smartphone-market-and-can

makers in China were Chinese: Huawei and Lenovo. By 2014, that number had increased to eight. Currently, all ten of China's largest-selling and popular smartphones are of Chinese origin.

Globally, Chinese brands today represent six of the world's ten largest-selling smartphones. Needless to say, Xiaomi is one of them, following closely on the heels of Samsung and Apple. Xiaomi founder Lei Jun likes to say, 'Even a pig can fly if it stands at the centre of a whirlwind.'[37] In a self-effacing manner, he is crediting Xiaomi's success to circumstances that came together. Jeffrey Towson, a private equity investor and a professor of business at Peking University in Beijing, said:

> 'Xiaomi was mostly in the right place at the right time, repeatedly. They emerged in China in 2012–2014 as smartphone adoption was growing dramatically. And by basically offering a cheaper iPhone-like, they rode that wave. Their strategy of innovative marketing plus Chinese manufacturing scale was a powerful combination at that time,'

But that is not all. It took some very persistent entrepreneurs, borderline obsessive behaviour, savvy marketing and a thorough understanding of the new generation of Chinese buyers for a company like Xiaomi to succeed against the odds. This is the unlikely story of Xiaomi, the people who built it, the strategies that worked for the company and the challenges it faces.

---

37 https://www.wsj.com/articles/xiaomi-chinas-new-phone-giant-takes-aim-at-world-1433731461

2

The Legend of Xiantao and One Last Roll of the Dice

IN THE SUMMER OF 2010, Xiaomi Corporation began its journey in a humble office in Zhongguancun, a technology hub in north-western Beijing, sometimes called China's Silicon Valley. Home-grown companies like Lenovo and multinationals such as Google, Intel and Microsoft have offices in this area that has seven technology parks and employs more than 2.7 million workers. It is walking distance from China's Peking University and a little further from Haidian Park, where you'll spot the latest of Chinese technology ranging from an autonomous vehicle to ferry passengers to a smart jogging track and an AI-based tai chi trainer.

In the early days, Xiaomi had only thirteen employees, including its eight co-founders (six engineers and two designers). The company's first and most illustrious employee, its primary founder Lei Jun, in his forties, was a battle hardy executive with the reputation as a hard-working entrepreneur and a successful angel investor. Over the years, Lei had earned the reputation of being a serial entrepreneur. Much of what Xiaomi is today is because of him.

Lei founded Xiaomi twelve years after he became the CEO of Kingsoft, the so-called Chinese Microsoft, in 1998. His entrepreneurial debut had happened more than six years previously, in the early nineties when he was a student at Wuhan University. Even though Xiaomi started at a time when China's domestic mobile phone industry was booming, it had the unique edge of Lei's enterprising genius and nearly two decades of experience running a company. So when the moment came, Lei was like an elite athlete with plenty of practice.

In 2008, years before the phenomena of 'building in public' became popular among start-ups, Lei started a personal blog to put down his thoughts on China's emerging mobile phone industry and reflect on global brands such as Apple and Microsoft. On 4 May 2009, he wrote: 'This year is a year of enthusiasm for the mobile internet. I have a bold guess: 2009 is the golden year of the mobile internet. The greatest mobile internet company in the next decade is either developed in 2009 or founded in 2009.'[1] Lei's prophecy came true on two counts—one, the Chinese smartphone company Vivo was founded in 2009 and has since met with great success, expanding to over 100 countries across the world and being ranked as one of the top ten smartphone brands since 2015. Two, at the time Lei was writing this, his own

---

1   http://leijun.blog.techweb.com.cn/ All quotations from Lei Jun's blog have been auto-translated from Chinese to working English. Much of the sentiment expressed in the blog may appear incongruous in English translation, but it has been kept intact to preserve the sanctity of the original text.

company Xiaomi was being developed. It launched soon after, on 6 April 2010.

Xiaomi's growth has happened at such an unprecedented speed that it continues to draw a lot of attention from journalists, users and industry insiders alike. Within two years of its launch, Xiaomi made it to Chinese internet giant Baidu's list of top five mobile phones.[2] This was especially significant since Xiaomi did not start off as a mobile handset company, choosing instead to launch itself as the company behind MIUI, an operating system based on Google's Android-operating system. Xiaomi officially entered the smartphone-making business in August 2011 when it announced the Mi1. After a waiting period of over two months, the phone went on sale.[3] With top-of-the-line specs, the Xiaomi Mi1 retailed at a cut price of about $310. It created quite a buzz in the market. Steven Millward at *Tech in Asia* called it the 'affordable dual-core beast'. Several others drew comparisons with the iPhone and other phones from brands such as HTC. With a large number of fans of its MIUI operating system already lined up (more on how Xiaomi built up a formidable army of Mi Fans in chapter 5) to buy the device, the launch couldn't have gone better. Over 300,000 pre-orders were placed in just 34 hours. However, there was one hitch.

Lei was accused of copying several aspects of the business from a company called Meizu.[4] According to a report published by online media company Tech in Asia, the founder of Meizu, Huang Zhang, aka J. Wong, wrote on the Meizu forum in August:

---

2   https://www.techinasia.com/baidu-report-reveals-top-webbrowsing-handset-models-china-911

3   https://www.gizmochina.com/2019/08/15/throwback-tech-thursday-xiaomi-first-smartphone-mi-1-revisited/

4   https://www.techinasia.com/xiaomi-vs-meizu

'I am not afraid of him, but I am simply sick of him. He used to pretend to be interested in investing in Meizu and approached me through his guanxi with leaders of the High Tech Zone. He got me to tell him all about how Meizu was running—from phone design, production, supply chain, marketing and even financial operation. He totally got me with his "sincerity". So do not talk about them, leave me alone, please!'[5]

Lei had met J. Wong several times since 2008 in the capacity of an investor. At the time, Meizu had already launched M8, an iPhone-like smartphone that ran on a modified Microsoft Windows-based operating system. Later in December, J. Wong fired another salvo on the Meizu forum:

'MIUI is a company funded by Lei Jun, including that browser, which seems to have been made out of the UC browser. After knowing all this, I feel regret for communicating with him on everything about Meizu. I even discussed the design doc of the M9UI with him. MIUI as a company is shameless, so please do not discuss anything about them here.'[6]

The two companies went toe to toe in the Chinese smartphone market in the early days. However, Meizu was soon relegated to the sidelines as Lei Jun went about executing Xiaomi's expansive strategy that has elements from several companies. The truth

---

5   Ibid.
6   Ibid.

is, a business can only copy a few aspects of another business, not all of it. Without internalizing why a feature or a particular decision was made, copying is indeed pointless. Seen from that lens, Xiaomi's success itself is proof that it is far more innovative than a 'shanzhai' company or a business that copied the blueprint from a competitor. American entrepreneur Jim McKelvey, who successfully defended his company Square against a competing product from Amazon and several other copycat products, puts it eloquently:

> 'So, if you look at the way an innovation stack evolves, the company that's inventing it is able to iterate very quickly and evolve this thing that eventually has 14 components. The company that's copying those 14 components has to copy all 14 components, and that's a totally different thing to do.'[7]

McKelvey puts forth that a company that is innovating is aware of the reasons why it is innovating, and a company that is merely copying does not understand the rationale. And without the rationale, a copycat finds it difficult to build on top of its failures and success. Xiaomi's drive to create new products and features comes from users and not from the need to copy from Apple or another successful company.

By 2013, with the Mi2 and Mi3 already in the market, Xiaomi had sold a staggering 18.7 million smartphones.[8] By

---

7   https://www.techinasia.com/xiaomi-vs-meizu

8   https://www.techinasia.com/xiaomi-sold-nearly-19-million-phones-in-2013

2014, Xiaomi was rapidly expanding into foreign markets—first Singapore, quickly followed by Malaysia, Philippines and India. At the time of writing the book, Xiaomi was available in over eighty countries across Asia, Africa, Europe, the Middle East and even the Americas. In 2018, Xiaomi made an initial public offering (IPO) at the HKSE, and in 2019 it became the youngest debutant on the Fortune Global 500 list. Xiaomi has consistently maintained a global image ranking as one of the top ten smartphone brands. In India, it emerged as the number one brand beating Samsung in 2017 and has retained its position for several quarters, with total sales crossing 100 million in September 2019.[9]

Xiaomi has achieved in less than a decade what most companies strive to accomplish in a lifetime. And much of that can be traced back to its CEO-founder Lei Jun. For all his failings in past roles, it is Lei's vision and lockstep execution at Xiaomi that made it the global brand that it is today.

> 'He was quite obviously the founder to watch at that time. He had assembled an all-star team around a strategy that seemed compelling, and Xiaomi had already built a grassroots fan base. Lei was one of a new generation of entrepreneurs who had seen what was possible with the C2C model and was now willing to push China forward as an innovator that could show the US a thing or two.'

Said Hamish McKenzie, the author of *Beta China: Dawn of an Innovation Generation*.

---

9   https://techcrunch.com/2018/01/25/xiaomi-samsung-india/

A lot of experience, past failures that came in the way of building a lasting legacy, and a hunger to taste truly lasting success are just some of the things that drove his manic focus on Xiaomi. It was his last bet, one last roll of the dice before he called it quits on entrepreneurship.

A fresh graduate aims high

Lei Jun was born in 1969 in Xiantao, located in central China's Hubei province. Until Lei became famous, Xiantao was mainly known as the 'gymnastics town', since it was home to several gymnastics' champions. Olympic gymnasts like Li Xiaoshuang, Yang Wei and Li Dashuang hail from the city. Years later, Lei would bring fame to the town not as a gymnast but as one of the country's most successful businessmen. Growing up, he was interested in poetry and loved to play Go. After graduating from Mianyang Middle School in 1987, Lei moved to Wuhan— also known as the Chicago of China, a bustling industrial city and the capital of Hubei—to attend college. Lei's father was a teacher and made about $7 a month.[10] Like millions of others who grew up in rural China in the eighties, doing well in studies was his ticket to a better world. So he worked hard and became an obedient student. In just two years, Lei graduated from Wuhan University, a top-tier institution in China, with a bachelor's degree in computer science that typically takes four years to complete.

Just as early access to computing had changed the lives of his heroes Bill Gates and Steve Jobs, computers also changed

---

10 https://time.com/5336633/lei-jun-xiaomi-trade-war/

Lei's life. Reminiscing about this generally exciting time as he slowly began discovering the marvels of computer technology, Lei later blogged, 'I found that the computer world was so beautiful that I plunged in.' Imagine a regular eighteen-year-old nerd obsessed with computers—Lei was no different. He rode 'a broken bicycle, carrying a large bag full of disks and reference books', and wandered the Wuhan Electric Street. Computer programming offered Lei a chance to escape the grim reality of the outside world. One day, he borrowed a book from the Wuhan University library that changed his outlook completely. The book was called *Fire in the Valley: The Making of the Personal Computer*, and it told the story of Steve Jobs and Steve Wozniak of Apple Computer Company and of Bill Gates of Microsoft and how they started a technological revolution. That day, the eighteen-year-old Lei made up his mind that he too, like his Silicon Valley heroes, would run a world-class company one day. It would take many years and some fortuitous events for that to happen. But the seeds of entrepreneurship were sown in his mind. Years later, Lei wrote about this in his blog in Chinese. It roughly translates to: 'The story of the heroes of Silicon Valley burned my chest all the time. I often dreamed that one day I would create a first-class software company. The whole world uses our software.'

Lei's late teens in the second half of the eighties coincided with a difficult period in Chinese history. The Communist Party of China, at the time led by Deng Xiaoping, started opening up the Chinese market in a bid to create a 'socialist society with Chinese characteristics'.

The government's decision in 1978 to introduce economic reforms after the death of Mao Zedong to lift China out of poverty had generated great enthusiasm and hope in the hearts of the Chinese public. Entrepreneurship was no longer treated with disdain and was even encouraged by the government.

> 'At that time, economic activity had been suspended for decades, and the social system was almost dead. The thundering call of Deng Xiaoping to reform and open up awakened the entire country, releasing its productive power and setting people free from rigid controls. The country had taken on a completely different appearance not long after the reform program started. Economic development was a mega trend, and speed and efficiency were defining the daily life of a billion people.'

Tian Tao, a member of Huawei International Advisory Board, and economics professor Wu Chunbo wrote in their book *The Huawei Story*.[11]

But even as China opened its markets by allowing large-scale privatization of former SoEs, in came massive corruption and nepotism. Soon, people realized that these reforms would only ever benefit a select few while imperilling the majority of China's population. When criticizing the government's policies did not yield effective results, the Chinese started mass demonstrations. Most notably, the Tiananmen Square protests of April 1989 in Beijing became so popular that the government had to declare martial law to shut them down. Hundreds of protestors were wounded and many others killed as the government cracked down on them. By then, the movement had spread like wildfire across 400 cities nationwide.

---

11 Tian Tao and Wu Chunbo, *The Huawei Story*. New Delhi: SAGE Publications, 2015.

Lei's hometown also took part in the 1989 protests. In April, thousands of students took to the streets of Wuhan demanding inflation control and an end to bureaucratic corruption. After the police crackdown in Tiananmen Square in June 1989, Wuhan University students blocked the railway tracks on the Beijing–Guangzhou line to condemn the police brutalities.[12] It appears that Lei took solace in computers. 'The computer is far less complicated than anyone else … Every time you sit in front of the computer, you are patrolling in your kingdom. Such a day is a heavenly day,' he later wrote in his blog, unrelated to the protests. As hobbies, Lei pursued philately and Go as well. But computers were much more than a hobby for him. Soon his passion for programming became a serious preoccupation.

During his sophomore summer vacation in August 1989, Lei co-wrote his first commercial software, the BITLOK, along with Wang Guoquan. Wang and Lei had met a few months ago on the electronics street and soon became best friends. They formed the Yellow Rose Group. The two worked day and night and wrote the original version of BITLOK in two weeks. It was an encryption software to help prevent piracy. Lei and Wang developed it for seven years until 1996 and sold it to several companies, including Yonyou and Kingsoft, earning 1 million yuan ($152,000).[13] Lei later called it his first 'bucket of gold'.

The second commercial programme Lei developed was an antivirus software called Immunity 90. He worked with his classmate Feng Zhihong during the winter vacation that year and

---

12 https://en.wikipedia.org/wiki/1989_Tiananmen_Square_protests

13 https://www.kindai.ac.jp/files/rd/research-center/management-innovation/kindai-management-review/vol3_7.pdf

wrote the programme in Pascal, an early programming language popular in the seventies and eighties. Lei wrote articles and gave lectures about computer viruses but didn't pursue the track for much longer. The duo also made RAMinit, a tool that cleared memory to improve the performance of the memory-starved computers of those days.

In 1990, Lei, Wang Guoquan and a couple of others started a company named sān sè (Three Colours) in a rented hotel room. The idea was to develop software that could translate Chinese to English. But they also did other things to make money—selling computers, typing, printing and so on. The bootstrapped company had little or no money but always came up with inventive ways to survive. Lei recalls in his blog that at times they'd send a colleague who was good at Mahjong to beat the cafeteria master and win meal tickets. 'That's how we live,' Lei wrote. The game of Mahjong, which involves skill, strategy and a bit of luck, was developed in China and is mostly played by four players. The venture failed, but years later, this resourcefulness would help in Xiaomi's early years. Three Colours didn't survive as differences cropped up among the partners and Lei and Wang decided to break free.

The two of them took a 286 PC and some small things that the company had and split. 'I think people grow up through setbacks and failures. Because of this failure, I have a clear understanding of my abilities, and I have made a down-to-earth, step-by-step mental preparation for future development,' Lei wrote in 2008. This was part of the training that would make Lei the elite entrepreneur that he is today.

Lei also has a competitive streak in him. An instance from his early life in college is illuminating. In Lei's biography, author

Chen Run writes that Lei gave up his habit of taking an afternoon nap because he was afraid others would leave him behind. 'I am particularly afraid of falling behind. Once I fall behind, I cannot catch up,' Lei is quoted as saying by Chen Run.

His love for programming became so great that Lei was certain this was all he wanted to do for the rest of his life. After graduation, he was dead set on going to Beijing while most of his classmates moved to Shenzhen, Guangzhou or the West.

The Tiananmen Square massacre of 1989 and the crackdown that followed had forced many to reconsider their future in China, and a large number of young Chinese left the country to pursue higher education in the US. From 1989 to 1994, the largest percentage of international students in the US was Chinese in origin. Xiaomi's current president and co-founder, Lin Bin, for instance, left to pursue a master's degree in computer science from Drexel University in the US. Similarly, Liu De, Xiaomi's senior vice president, went to the Art Centre College of Design in California to study industrial design. Unlike his peers, Lei was not interested in institutionalized and structured forms of learning. Besides, much as programming fascinated the young Lei, he knew it would take years for China to get to a place where it could be taken seriously. In his blog, Lei lamented, 'At the beginning, we felt that we had nothing to do, and even more terrible is that we are particularly smart, especially suitable for developing software, much stronger than foreigners ...' And while things looked bleak at the time, both in terms of China's socio-political climate as well as its technological future, the optimist in him knew that change would surely come and that he, Lei, the budding programmer and founder of Yellow Rose Software Team, was certainly going to be at the forefront of that grand transformation. 'Not only does Lei Jun love programming, but he is also a perfectionist. He writes code like writing poetry, like flowing clouds and flowing water,' Lei's biographer wrote.[14]

A complex journey begins

After a chance meeting with Qiu Bojun, the founder of Kingsoft, at a computer exhibition in Beijing, Lei was offered a job at Kingsoft. Lei, already known for his programming expertise, joined the company in 1992, fresh out of university, and became the head of its research and development department. Kingsoft's founder Kau Pak Kwan aka Qiu Bojun had big plans of making his company the best in the software industry. Qiu was quite the legend in the Chinese software industry. The origin myth is that back in 1988, twenty-four-year-old Qiu had worked non-stop on a 386 computer for some 17 months to write 122,000 lines of code in assembly language that went into the first Chinese language word processor.[15] It was an instant bestseller and laid the groundwork for Kingsoft to become a top tech company in China.

Lei, all of twenty-three, was instantly captivated by Qiu's aspirations and mastery of programming. Thus began Lei's complex journey at Kingsoft and one that was largely responsible for moulding him into the person that he is today. But Lei also suffered severe setbacks at Kingsoft. Chief among them was the

---

14 Chen Run, *Lei Jun Biography*. Wuhan: Huazhong University Press, 2013.

15 https://books.google.co.in/books?id=24P3M4hrpWwC&pg=PA140&lpg
=PA140&dq=Qiu+Bojun+wrote+non+stop&source=bl&ots=yzllAllh8R&
sig=ACfU3U2FD0LLkEFSYYHTbCWwa2VYwCi2YQ&hl=en&sa=X&
ved=2ahUKEwjw48miwPjoAhU9xDgGHd0oBT4Q6AEwAHoECAo
QAQ#v=onepage&q=Qiu%20Bojun%20wrote%20non%20stop&f=false

doomed product called Pangu Office, an office management product on which Lei and his team spent nearly three years. Pangu was a failure and lost money and almost bankrupted Kingsoft. Defeated, Lei tendered his resignation in April 1996. Instead of letting Lei go, Qiu gave him six months of leave. Lei, who was twenty-seven years old at the time, soon recovered from the burnout and went back to work at Kingsoft in November that year.

Kingsoft raised $4.5 million from Lenovo in 1998 to mount an offensive against Microsoft.[16] And at the ridiculously young age of twenty-nine, Lei became Kingsoft's CEO. Kingsoft was China's very own Microsoft, which meant its products were strikingly similar to the MS Office suite and included a word processor, spreadsheet and presentation programmes—all in Chinese. Afterwards, it also developed its own antivirus and cloud storage facilities. At the time Lei became Kingsoft's CEO, the company was already facing double troubles—both at home and from outside. As the Chinese Microsoft, Kingsoft was not only facing stiff foreign competition, but thriving software piracy in China almost bankrupted it. Kingsoft was not the only company to be plagued by piracy; the issue had, in fact, crippled the entire Chinese tech industry. In 2006, the tech magazine *Wired* wrote, 'Losses to piracy are especially damaging at a time when communist leaders want China to transform itself from the world's low-cost factory into an "innovation society" that makes its own profitable technology and brand names.'[17] Although Kingsoft's software was installed on most computers,

---

16   https://technology-info.net/index.php/2019/11/20/lei-juns-jinshan-past/
17   https://www.wired.com/2006/07/piracy-zaps-chinas-tech-industry/

the company was not making any money. Nearly 90 per cent of the installations were pirated copies. For a company that prided itself as the 'preferred alternative to Microsoft Office', it was becoming increasingly clear that just being an 'alternative' was not good enough.

In these dark days, as the company's chief, Lei decided to hold a workshop to motivate his employees. He shared some nuggets of wisdom that he had curated over the years by closely following successful US-based companies such as Google, Apple and Microsoft. Recreating a moment straight out of high school, Lei asked his co-workers to recite the two magic words after him—'focus' and 'extreme'.

'Google and Apple are great,' Lei later wrote in his blog, 'because they have the focus and the ultimate gene. Starting from the beginning of entrepreneurship, entrepreneurs have the opportunity to make a company as great as Google and Apple if they insist on "focus" and "extreme"!'

In his effort to improve Kingsoft, Lei also tried adopting Microsoft's policy of providing the best user experience. 'The secret of Microsoft's success lies in the user experience, not only to solve user needs but also to make users feel easy to use … The key factor in the success of internet products is user word of mouth.' Unfortunately, despite Lei's best efforts, Kingsoft could not fulfil its founder Qiu Bojun's dreams of becoming the best in the software industry.

But Lei's ideas and gathered wisdom did not ultimately go to waste. In a few years, he once again put these ideas into motion as he prepared to launch Xiaomi. Only, this time, he had a playbook and it worked like a charm. Under Lei's leadership, Xiaomi has striven to offer the best user experience in the market. Xiaomi's regular feature updates are a reflection of how much it values user feedback, and for this alone it continues to receive praise from users and industry insiders alike. But let's not get ahead of ourselves.

Back in the early noughties when Lei was still the CEO of Kingsoft, and the idea of Xiaomi was not even born, he frequently found himself at a dead end. Caught between the piracy of Kingsoft's products at home and the stiff competition from abroad, Lei decided to diversify its products by launching antivirus, gaming and translation software. Once again, Lei's efforts did not pay off, and Kingsoft continued to struggle. Later, in 2012, following Lei's great success with his new company Xiaomi, *Forbes* did a retrospective feature on Lei's 'long, twisting road' at Kingsoft, perhaps to familiarize readers with his career trajectory. It described Lei as being frequently 'exhausted and lost' for despite the hardships and excruciating work pressure at Kingsoft, 'the results were not satisfactory'.[18] Like with most other things, filing Kingsoft's IPO also proved to be a challenge. When it was ultimately listed in 2007 after several unsuccessful attempts, a battle-worn Lei took it as a cue to step down as CEO and channel his energy elsewhere. Some sixteen years and several bruising battles later, Lei was tired. But he'd soon embark on a journey as an angel investor and see tremendous success.

Looking into the future and playing angel

Lei's journey at Kingsoft may well have been long and twisted, but during his time there, he also dabbled in various other ventures.

---

18 https://www.forbes.com/sites/laurahe/2012/07/19/chinese-billionaire-lei-juns-long-twisting-road-at-kingsoft/#2b8be0ac6b82

His first brush with the internet was in 1993, at the Institute of High Energy Physics in China. That was China's first internet line. But it wasn't until the late nineties that he would catch on to the internet's possibilities. In 1999, backed by Kingsoft, Lei launched Joyo, a website that allowed people to download software and sought to make money from advertising. But that didn't work out, and in 2000, Joyo pivoted to an e-commerce site selling mainly books, software and music. With Joyo, Lei gained first-hand experience in e-commerce, slowly familiarizing himself with the nitty-gritty of handling huge online demands. Could Lei have been preparing himself for future flash sales that would see thousands of Xiaomi phones fly off the (virtual) shelves in a matter of a few seconds? Most likely. Clay Shirky, author of *Little Rice: Smartphones, Xiaomi, and the Chinese Dream*, writes about the time when Lei started testing an early version of Joyo's e-commerce platform through an interesting experiment. By selling cans of Coke to Joyo employees at a reduced price of 1 mao (roughly 1.5 cents) per can instead of the actual price of 1 yuan (roughly 15 cents), Lei wanted to check if Joyo's platform would be able to support the sudden spurt in demand. Shirky observes, 'Lei Jun had a great appreciation for the odd dynamics of e-commerce from his days at Joyo, where the peak number of transactions a site can be asked to perform is a significant multiple of the median load.'[19]

Joyo's rise soon caught the attention of the American e-commerce giant Amazon. For Jeff Bezos, founder and CEO of Amazon, Joyo represented not just a large online retail

---

19 Clay Shirky, *Little Rice: Smartphones, Xiaomi, and the Chinese Dream*. New York: Columbia Global Reports, 2015.

platform but the key that would help Amazon unlock the
Chinese market. In 2004, Amazon acquired Joyo for $75 million
and major shareholders, including Kingsoft, Lenovo and Tiger
Management, cashed out.[20] In a press release, Bezos said, 'We are
very pleased to be entering the Chinese market with Joyo.com.
In a relatively short time, Joyo.com has established itself as the
leading online destination for books, music, and videos in China,
and we're happy to be part of one of the world's most dynamic
markets.' Lei, founder and chairman at Joyo, in his turn said,
'This transaction is a recognition of Joyo's accomplishments over
the past four years. I am confident that Amazon.com's expertise
in global e-commerce, in combination with Joyo's entrepreneurial
management team and employees, will bring the development of
e-commerce and online customer experience in China to a new
level.' The acquisition helped Amazon get a foothold in China
and offer services to over 80 million Chinese consumers who were
already online and hungry for imported luxury items. Following
the buyout, Joyo was renamed as Amazon.cn at first and later
changed again from Joyo Amazon to Amazon China. Despite
gaining an early entry into one of the world's biggest emerging
markets, Amazon's China experience was far from pleasant. It
perpetually found itself at a natural disadvantage against local
giants such as Alibaba and JD.com; even the super-profitable
Amazon Prime day sales paled in comparison to Alibaba's Singles
Day revenue earnings. In the summer of 2019, after struggling to
gain a foothold for fifteen years, Bezos decided to pull Amazon

---

20 http://www.internetnews.com/bus-news/article.php/3397241/
    Amazon+Acquires+Chinese+Joyo.htm

out of the Chinese market and focus on India instead.[21] Amazon's Chinese fairy tale may not have had a happy ending, but its $75 million acquisition of Joyo certainly propelled Lei into the big league.

Joyo was the first of Lei's series of successful business ventures, but it is important to remember that his ambitions were never limited to the companies he founded or even to those that he invested in. Rather, since a very early age, Lei was focused on bigger goals and, with every move, he has striven towards achieving them. Lei, together with Alibaba founder Jack Ma and Tencent's Pony Ma, has often been called 'China's disruptor' for radically changing how China is perceived today by the rest of the world. As the heads of some of the highest-grossing companies in the world, these Chinese entrepreneurs have helped the country shake off its image as the land of dingy sweatshops and cheap knock-offs, instead presenting China in its new avatar as the fastest-growing economy in the world since the economic reforms of 1978. This transformation from cheap China to the formidable superpower, of course, did not happen by chance but was a culmination of years of calculated thinking and ambitious planning by some of the country's greatest minds including Lei.

In 2001, after the dot-com bubble burst, the Chinese government decided to send executives of a few software companies on a mission to India to learn how its neighbour was managing its information industries. This was Lei's first visit to India as the representative of Jinshan (Jinshan Ruanjian was the Chinese name for Kingsoft, which literally translates to Gold Mountain Software). While first-world economies suffered from

---

21 https://www.nytimes.com/2019/04/18/technology/amazon-china.html

the NASDAQ crash following the dot-com bubble, India had surprisingly managed to stay on course. This was because of many reasons: India had already developed into a 'digital Eden' with computer training schools, generous foreign investments and programmers somewhat proficient in English.[22] Besides, Indian outsourcing software companies such as Infosys had thousands of programmers working for extremely low pay. In comparison, China's local companies were small-time enterprises that were bleeding because of domestic piracy problems. Chinese emissaries such as Lei hoped that their mission to India would help them tide over these crises.

China's fortunes turned shortly thereafter when, in the early noughties, internet cafés mushroomed, offering China's poorer masses cheap access to the internet. Until then, only wealthy families could afford home computers while the rest of the country was oblivious to the marvels of information technology. Thanks to the proliferation of internet cafés and China's thriving piracy industry, the country's young population was quickly hooked to online games. Nationwide, Chinese parents lamented their children's obsession with games, but little did anyone realize how these games were inadvertently helping millions of Chinese young adults learn the fundamentals of operating computers. China may not have had professional schools like India to train future programmers, but the boom in cyber hubs and the gaming culture did create a generation of computer enthusiasts. The popularity of the online games culture, of course, reflected in the number of game users. Lei, who had been closely watching

---

22 https://mp.weixin.qq.com/s/Hx6ePqgTRYWEJSkR5nlJZw?fbclid= IwAR1cRYSGFOymeFnGId_GvK_tzb7AKkaludBP8F6SDE_ VgItKUSzgyD8er-w

this new development, noted on his blog how China registered a 22.9 per cent hike in online gamers between 2007 and 2008. In 2008, there were 49.3 million users, and the gaming industry generated revenues worth 150 million yuan ($22.8 million). At this time, Kingsoft itself had a 2.69 per cent share in the game market. In 2010, Kingsoft invested in Cheetah Mobile (formerly called Kingsoft Network), a company that develops popular online games apart from other entertainment applications. Lei, who acted as Cheetah's chairman until 2018, also owns personal shares in the company.

Once Kingsoft filed its IPO on the HKSE in 2007, Lei decided to step down as its CEO and devote all his energy to angel investments. He had been grappling with the idea of the internet for a long time, but by the early noughties, Lei had figured that the future was going to be all about the mobile internet. Acting upon that intuition, Lei began to invest money in internet companies. In fact, Lei began investing in promising start-ups even before he had resigned as Kingsoft's CEO. In November 2006, Lei met his friend Yu Yongfu at a bar for drinks. At the time, Lei was still running the show at Kingsoft. Yu, part of an investing firm, was unable to convince the other partners to invest in a mobile web start-up called UCWeb. Yu and Lei were not just friends, they also had shared views regarding China's technological future. Like Lei, Yu too believed that after Japan, it was soon going to be China's turn to ride the mobile internet revolution. Yu convinced Lei to invest in UC. Lei agreed to do it on the condition that Yu would become the CEO of UCWeb. In just a few months, Lei raised $10 million and the company's value increased tenfold. In just another year, while returning from UC's annual board meeting, Yu would once again persuade Lei to take on more responsibilities and yet again Lei could not turn down his offer. So, on 16 October 2008, Lei became the chairman of UCWeb's board of directors. The environment at UCWeb was already electric since the company had clocked a twenty-five times growth in active users so that now people truly believed that they could become the next Google. Upon assuming office, Lei gave a speech at UCWeb's strategy conference where he spoke about the company's tremendous potential and the unstoppable force that is the mobile internet. He said, 'UCWeb's dream is that every Chinese user can use UCWeb, which can help everyone put the internet in their pockets, and is committed to promoting the great cause of the entire mobile internet.'

By 2008, Lei was mostly dabbling in angel investments, but he did not feel fully prepared to take the plunge and become a full time investor. On 24 October 2008, Lei wrote on his blog, 'I did think about being a professional investor and being a "real capitalist" but I am not ready yet.' Even so, from very early on, Lei knew how to be generous yet restrained in his investments, which is to say that he was giving in terms of capital and support but exercised restraint when it came to thrusting his opinions on someone else.

As an angel investor, Lei picked some winners including Vancl, UCWeb and Lakala by following the mantra that if 'the big direction is good, the small direction is verified, the team is excellent,' then 'the return on investment is high'. He also thought that teams should be tuned to user needs and sensitive to the market, down-to-earth and have two or three people with complementary skills. They should have a technology co-founder, be fast to execute at low cost, have experience if possible, and they should be playing in a big market. They should be well-timed, the teams should focus and should have tried out the opportunity on a smaller scale.

Over time, he helped many start-ups get on their feet, thereby creating an ecosystem that fostered growth in the field of e-commerce and the mobile internet. Take Vancl, for example. A top online clothing retailer in China, Vancl was founded in 2007 and had Lei as one of its primary angel investors. Similarly, in 2005, Lei also helped raise capital for YY Inc., a video-sharing social media platform. YY Inc. went on to list on the NASDAQ. In 2010, Lei started a venture capital firm called Shunwei Capital with Tuck Lye Koh to help China's fresh crop of internet companies with early and mid-stage investments. Lei was quick to realize that China had only a few angel investors, with most investors wanting to come in during the later stage private equity rounds when risk is lower. In 2016, at the 'New Normal, New Idea, New Kinetic Energy' forum at Davos, Lei discussed the pros and cons of angel investment. He said:

'Angel investors spot trends and opportunities, and I saw the future in mobile internet. As entrepreneurs, we have to ask ourselves what will happen in five years, what will be the trend in ten years? What is the right thing to do? When is the right time? My role as an investor is to look into the future, spot trends and opportunities.'[23]

In 2016, Lei's angel investment tips certainly carried a lot of weight since he had just made a 1,000x return on his investments in UCWeb. Back in 2007, after that fateful night at the bar with

---

23 https://kr-asia.com/voices-leijun-i-saw-the-future-in-mobile-internet

his friend Yu Yongfu, Lei had invested about $600,000 for 20 per cent of UCWeb. When Alibaba acquired the company for $4.3 billion in 2014, Lei turned his $600,000 into $860,000,000, a profit of over 1,000x.[24]

Lei was restless after Kingsoft, even though he'd become a successful investor. He still wanted to build a company large enough and successful enough to match his outsized ambition. So in 2010, Lei founded Xiaomi Corporation. By then, he had become a veteran, having spent over twenty years as an industry insider and over a decade as an entrepreneur.

Xiaomi was truly a culmination of Lei's long years of experience that had led him to believe that the future lay in the mobile internet. It was clear to him that the mobile phone and the internet will be two of the largest trends shaping lives in the future. His years as a successful angel investor had also earned him the admiration and respect of colleagues. One such person was Richard Liu, co-founder of Morningside Venture Capital. Like Lei, Liu too had invested in UCWeb and YY, among other companies. The first time Lei got on a phone call with Liu about Xiaomi, they stayed up the whole night exchanging ideas. When Lei finally hung up, it was already morning and he knew he had found an investor in his friend Liu. In January 2010, Lei Jun talked to Hans Tung, the managing partner at GGV Capital, a multi-stage venture capital firm with $3.8 billion in capital under management. GGV Capital also became a Xiaomi backer.

---

24 https://c.mi.com/thread-2014721-1-0.html

Years later, at an interview at Draper University, US, Liu would recall the early days at Xiaomi.[25] We may perhaps never know what exactly Lei and Liu talked about that night, but Liu's interview throws some light on what motivated these two individuals to build something challenging with Xiaomi. Like many of Lei's peers who left China in the years following Tiananmen Square, Lui too had moved to America to attend college. His years at Cornell and later at the Massachusetts Institute of Technology (MIT) not only sharpened his business acumen, but also exposed him to the larger American society. Liu realized that the American economy had been shaped by the baby boomers, the generation born in the years after the World War II. These boomers, with their modes of consumption, had helped build the American economy. But the story of America was not very far removed from Liu's own reality. Much like the baby boomers, there was a similar generation that had grown up in the years following China's epochal Cultural Revolution—the post-Cultural Revolution generation, as he liked to call them—who were going to help shape the Chinese economy. Liu was not wrong; since the economic reforms led to the opening up of its market, China had begun proactively participating in globalization for the first time in the nation's history. Of the 1.3 billion Chinese population, around 300 million to 400 million currently belong to the middle class, with experts estimating the number to exceed 700 million in the next few years. Imagine a country with a 700+ million population with easy, disposable income and a penchant for luxury goods and you are, in fact, imagining China's future as the most powerful consumer market

25 https://www.youtube.com/watch?v=TIPdsQ8lBKI&t=335s

in the world. People like Richard Liu and Lei Jun were quick to realize this, and they were even quicker to put their thoughts into action, which made Xiaomi such a revolutionary company.

The second investor Jun called, Hans Tung of GGV Capital, was at first shocked at Lei Jun's vision. 'In the first half an hour, I was in complete shock,' Tung recalled in an interview in 2018 after Xiaomi's public offering. To him, no phone company had started from scratch and succeeded in the recent past. Lei's pitch was around his conviction about smartphones becoming the most common computing device people would use, and that new brands will be built and sold online and in close collaboration with consumers online. On top of that, Lei Jun also didn't want to make profits from hardware, but he had his sights on monetizing through internet services. Tung eventually saw sense in that and decided to invest. Tung recalled in the 2018 interview ' … no one else in China had similar thoughts at that point in time. It was designed to be more customer friendly than existing hardware players at the time and also more integrated than any internet service company in China was willing to do.'

Striking gold: customer feedback

As a fan of Steve Jobs and the iPhone, Lei Jun could clearly see that smartphones were the future. In 2010, at the age of forty, he wanted to cement his legacy with a truly great company. To that end, he started Xiaomi. Lei had initially launched the brand in the form of an Android-based operating system called MIUI. All those years of fiddling with mobile phones had made Lei keenly aware of their shortcomings. In the closing years of the noughties, when Nokia was gasping for breath and the market was being flooded with phones from Samsung, HTC and Motorola, Lei realized that despite their high price, these phones had an average-quality operating system and customers wanted a better experience. The MIUI operating system was undoubtedly a finer product, but there was another problem. Replacing the original operating system with MIUI needed technical skills; if done wrong, it could make the handset unusable. But by then, the superior quality of the MIUI had earned it a community of fans who would risk it anyway. Xiaomi's long association with its fans perhaps dates back to this moment when these fans put their trust in a brand-new product that had no prior industry accreditation.

They were not disappointed. Lei's years at Kingsoft had taught him the virtues of customer feedback. In Kingsoft's R&D department, he was always surrounded by engineers. The company did not have a marketing department, so the job of answering calls from customers fell on Lei. This was a refreshing experience—it made Lei realize how valuable user feedback is in addressing problems promptly. Now at Xiaomi, Lei used the same strategy, focusing minutely on every piece of feedback they received from MIUI users and delivering weekly updates instead of yearly updates as was the industry norm at the time. Xiaomi's earliest MIUI users became its most prized resource, spreading the word about the product's excellence so that when Xiaomi launched its first handset in 2011, it organically created the hype and publicity that few others had generated in the history of the industry. Part of its grand plan was to sell phones at 'honest prices'. To that end, Lei told his employees that he wanted to make and sell great-performing smartphones at only $300 while competing models would have cost nearly $600.[26] Clearly, the strategy worked.

For Lei, the switch to hardware was as exciting as it was daunting since this was unfamiliar territory but one that he was ready to explore. This also gave him a chance to put together a team that would help in successfully integrating the hardware, the software and the internet. Over time, Lei convinced the best minds in each field to come and join him at Xiaomi. Some were old colleagues from Kingsoft, while others had formerly held important positions at Google, Motorola and Samsung. Although Xiaomi was founded in April 2010, Lei had started laying the groundwork for the company almost a year before. In 2009, Lei met his first co-founder Lin Bin through Kai Fu Lee, the Taiwanese American computer scientist who was the head of Google in China.[27] Lin Bin, vice president of the Google China Institute of Engineering, was tasked with localizing Android for the Chinese market. Both Lei and Lin Bin shared an obsession with the mobile phone and spent hours chatting about it after work. When Kai-Fu Lee quit Google in 2009, and later Google announced its intention to quit the China market altogether, Lin Bin chose to join Lei in his pursuit to build a world-class mobile company from China. Li Wanqiang, the other co-founder at Xiaomi came from Kingsoft. Li, who had worked with Lei for several years, had burnt out and made plans to pursue photography. That was when Lei asked him to join Xiaomi, where he would take charge of marketing and branding. Meanwhile, Lin Bin roped in Huang Jiangi, his former colleague at Microsoft, and

---

26 http://cnbj1.fds.api.xiaomi.com/company/financial/en-US/IPO.pdf

27 Chen Run, *Lei Jun Biography*, Huazhong University Press, 2013.

Hong Feng, who reported to him at Google, as the fourth and fifth co-founders. Lei also convinced Liu De, who returned to China after graduating in industrial design from the Art Center College of Design in California, to establish the Industrial Design Department at the Beijing University of Technology, to join Xiaomi. The team still didn't have anyone with serious hardware chops. After interviewing dozens of candidates and drawing a blank, on a whim they decided to approach Zhou Guangping, a fifty-five-year-old Motorola veteran. As luck would have it, Zhou agreed. Lei had also invited his friend Wang Chuan, who initially refused but changed his mind in 2012 and joined Xiaomi.

It was Lei's obsession with perfecting the 'triathlon model' of the business that encompasses hardware, software and internet services that got Xiaomi its next big investor. In 2011, Russia's most influential tech investor Yuri Milner of DST Global was looking to invest in China, having recently moved DST's headquarters from Moscow to Hong Kong. Milner was a name to reckon with in the tech industry with stakes in AirBnB, Twitter, Spotify, Snapchat and Facebook. He had already met with Alibaba's Jack Ma way back in 2005 and in 2010 had taken a five-hour flight from Moscow to Beijing to meet Richard Liu, Xiaomi's earliest investor, to discuss Liu's new project, Jingdong 360. Besides Jingdong, Milner was also interested in Liu's portfolio and in the companies he had angel funded in the recent past. Thanks to Richard Liu, in September 2011, at a time when Xiaomi had just announced its first smartphone but was still days away from making any actual sales, Milner visited Lei in his tiny Xiaomi office and sat down for a quick chat. At that moment, Xiaomi was no more than a risky venture, but it was Lei's confidence and his determination to excel in all three aspects of the business that appealed to Milner the most. As a seasoned investor, Milner knew he had to get in there before Xiaomi got too big.[28]

On Milner's recommendation, DST invested $500 million over multiple rounds, including three exclusive rounds, and bought 7 per cent of the company's shares. Milner's genuine interest in Xiaomi and in its leader, in particular, was the shot in the arm that Lei needed at this point. It assured him that he might indeed be on to something. Earlier that year, Lei had spoken at an interview about his plans with Xiaomi. The interviewer had asked Lei about his future plans in case Xiaomi did not succeed. There was nothing odd about the question. After all, Lei was a serial entrepreneur and start-ups were known to fail from time to time. The interviewer had merely wondered what Lei might have planned next in case Xiaomi failed to take off. Lei responded in his characteristic candid manner; without mincing any words, he said,

'No, this is the last time, even if I lose. Because I have tried it, I tried it when I was forty years old, I was strong, and I had all the social resources. If I lose, then I will quit. So when we started, we told everyone clearly that we would work together for four years. If we couldn't get it within four years, we would withdraw.'[29]

It was the last roll of the dice.

---

28 https://www.forbes.com/sites/parmyolson/2015/03/25/yuri-milners-unparalleled-global-tech-gold-mining-machine/#1366690c7d9b

29 From Lei's blog.

Ever since college, Lei had dreamt of running a world-class company. His days at Jinshan were long and busy, but they did not bring him much fulfilment. When he was not fighting off piracy on the domestic front, he was busy plotting strategies to protect Kingsoft from Microsoft's competition. He was young then, and the initial challenges did not bother him much. But over time, as it became clear that Kingsoft's problems would not abate, Lei began looking for an exit strategy. His growing interest in the emerging mobile internet industry offered some solace, as did his engagements as an angel advisor in China's upcoming internet companies. Yet, his plans of running a world-class company remained a distant dream. When Xiaomi finally happened, Lei was already forty, which was just the right age if he were to nurture his baby company to the heights of success. However, if this venture were to fail, Lei knew it was too late to start something all over again. Quitting under such circumstances was not the impulsive move of an embittered founder but rather the sign of a pragmatic entrepreneur gracefully bowing out of the race.

Luckily for Lei, the occasion to quit the game never arose. Xiaomi became Lei's dark horse as it exceeded everyone's expectations and quickly became one of China's most-loved smartphone brands. Until then, Lei had been a renowned figure in China's tech scene, but as Xiaomi started creating ripples in the mobile phone industry, the Western media sat up to take notice of the company's maverick founder. When Lei entered the big billionaires' club in 2012, *Forbes* ran two stories, both headlines insinuating Lei was China's very own Steve Jobs. One headline read, 'Meet Lei Jun: China's Steve Jobs is the Country's Newest Billionaire', while the other read, 'Xiaomi's Lei Jun:

China's Answer to Steve Jobs?' This was just the beginning; in 2014 *Forbes Asia* crowned Lei businessman of the year. Lei had also emerged as the eighth-richest man in China, worth $9.9 billion.[30] According to the *Forbes* report, 'Xiaomi's sales in the first half of 2014 hit $5.5 billion, surpassing all of 2013, when, according to a loan document seen by the Wall Street Journal, it netted $566 million.'[31] Lei, who by now was a lot more certain of Xiaomi's continued success, told *Forbes Asia*, 'If I said four years ago I would do this, I would have had no credibility.'

As China's newest billionaire sensation, Lei did receive a lot of good press. But he did not get to hog the limelight all by himself; with each story, Lei's comparisons with Apple's iconic founder Steve Jobs grew. As someone who had grown up idolizing Jobs, this may have been flattering at first. But as more and more business and tech journals started featuring Lei, newer resemblances were drawn up between the two personalities. Even back home, Lei is often called 'Leibs', a portmanteau made up of Lei and Jobs. Critics have commented on Lei's sartorial choices—black t-shirt, black trousers—much like Jobs' attire of black mock turtleneck and blue jeans; they have even discussed how the two had accomplished similar goals in their respective careers. Yet, these comparisons did not remain limited to Lei and Jobs. Xiaomi, which had striven to produce high-spec, low-price phones, was being dubbed an Apple knock-off, much like its founder, who was himself a Jobs copycat. While no one at Xiaomi has ever explicitly admitted to 'copying' Apple's iPhones, Lei has variously

---

30 https://www.forbes.com/sites/russellflannery/2014/12/03/the-disruptor/#1589c0373948

31 Ibid.

expressed a range of emotions at the ceaseless comparisons. In his blog, Lei once wrote, 'If you said that I am Jobs II in my twenties, I will feel happy, but when I was in my forties, [if] you said that I am the second (Jobs), I think it is a joke. I only need to be the first in the Lei Jun [category].' At Xiaomi, one unwritten rule is that if a Xiaomi product is kept next to an Apple product, it should not look out of place, a former Xiaomi employee said.

3

Going Places with an All-star Player

WITHIN YEARS OF ITS launch, Xiaomi earned itself a prime position as a distinguished Chinese brand. Its high-specs, low-price feature immediately hit a sweet spot among the price-sensitive yet brand-conscious consumers in China. By mid 2013, barely two years after it had sold its first smartphone, Xiaomi had shipped 10 million devices. Xiaomi's rapid growth propelled Lei into the league of billionaires. As per *Forbes*, by March 2013, his net worth was $1.8 billion. His wealth grew more than five times to $9.2 billion by the end of April 2020. *Forbes* estimates his net worth to be over $24.9 billion as of 24 November 2020. Lei was ranked at 147 in the *Forbes* billionaires list, and he was the twenty-fifth-richest man in China.[1] In 2014, *Forbes Asia* recognized him as businessman of the year. In October 2013, Taiwan-based market analyst TrendForce reported that

---

1   https://www.forbes.com/profile/lei-jun/#547a84b76e64

Xiaomi had outperformed HTC to emerge as the fifth-most-used smartphone in China. By the last quarter of 2013, overall sales had touched 18.7 million. The next year, Xiaomi became the largest-selling smartphone in China. Once Xiaomi devices took China by storm, Lei realized it was time to enter new markets.

Surging domestic sales alone could hardly have powered Xiaomi's global ambitions. Lei's entrepreneurship and deep knowledge of China's domestic market helped make Xiaomi China's favourite smartphone brand, but the journey ahead needed an international hand. The appointment of Hugo Barra as vice president of Xiaomi Global in 2013 signalled a new chapter in the company's history. If the game is the business of smartphones, then Barra was clearly an all-star player. Barra, who had been a senior executive at Google—the vice president of Android product management—was touted as a 'significant hire' not just because of the sheer magnitude of roles and duties he was expected to perform as vice president of Xiaomi's future global relations but also because he was the very first non-Chinese senior official to be welcomed into the Xiaomi family.[2] The task of Xiaomi's global expansion was now placed squarely on Barra's shoulders. Lin Bin, co-founder and president of Xiaomi, said it was entirely Barra's job 'to figure out which region we should enter next and how'.[3]

Outside the immediate context of Xiaomi's organic growth model, Lei's vision of global expansion also coincided with China's grandiose global development strategy. In 2013, Xi

2   https://en.wikipedia.org/wiki/Hugo_Barra
3   https://thenextweb.com/asia/2013/09/09/xiaomi-co-founder-on-why-ex-google-exec-barra-and-its-own-firmware-are-key-to-international-success/

Jinping, the supreme leader of the People's Republic of China, during his official visit to Indonesia and Kazakhstan, made the first public announcement about China's novel One Belt One Road initiative. The large-scale infrastructure venture would let China grow its trade and invest in over 152 countries and international organizations across the world.[4] The ambitious project, comprising extensive highways and railways at an estimated cost of over $1 trillion, is slated for a 2049 completion to commemorate the 100th anniversary of the Chinese republic. The Chinese government claims that the main aim of the initiative is 'to construct a unified large market and make full use of both international and domestic markets through cultural exchange and integration, to enhance mutual understanding and the trust of member nations, ending up in an innovative pattern with capital inflows, talent pool, and technology database'.[5] Given the project's sheer scale and budget, admirers have hailed it as Xi Jinping's twenty-first-century rendition of the historic Silk Road, the all-important trade route between the East and the West up until the eighteenth century.

The project could potentially be the biggest driver of Chinese exports after containerization revolutionized shipping and put globalization on steroids. Economist and journalist Marc Levinson perhaps has the most interesting take on containerization. In his book *The Box: How the Shipping Container Made the World Smaller and the World Economy Bigger*,[6] he tells the story of how containers revolutionized international trade. After the invention

---

4   https://en.wikipedia.org/wiki/Belt_and_Road_Initiative
5   Ibid.
6   Marc Levinson, *The Box: How the Shipping Container Made the World Smaller and the World Economy Bigger*. New Jersey: Princeton University Press, 2008.

of uniform metal containers in 1956 by American businessman Malcom McLean, the cost of shipping fell drastically. McLean's calculations pointed to the fact that it cost only $0.16 per tonne to load containers compared with $5.83 per tonne for loose cargo. This increased cross-border trade many times over. As the *Economist* points out, a study of twenty-two industrialized countries showed a 320 per cent increase in bilateral trade in the five years leading up to 2013 and a 790 per cent increase in the twenty years to 2013.[7]

Containerization tipped the scales in favour of countries where manufacturing labour was cheaper, and China was its biggest beneficiary. About a third of all containers in the world pass through ports in China, and the country has seven of the world's top ten ports. World Bank data from 2018 shows that of the 792 million containers that moved across the world, China had the biggest share with about 225 million containers, followed by the US at 55 million containers.[8] The One Belt One Road initiative is expected to boost trade even further.

If Xi's Silk Road initiative created a stir in geopolitical circles with speculations over China's imminent dominance of global trade and commerce, the Western tech world was abuzz with news of Barra's recent move to Beijing to work at an obscure Chinese smartphone company. To be sure, even gizmo freaks and tech gurus from Europe and the US who had checked out Xiaomi's products during trips to China and were blown away by its high-specs, low-price phones, still struggled with the brand's name. Leading

7   https://www.economist.com/the-economist-explains/2013/05/21/why-have-containers-boosted-trade-so-much

8   https://data.worldbank.org/indicator/IS.SHP.GOOD.TU?most_recent_value_desc=true

news broadcasters and dailies such as the BBC, CNBC and the *Economic Times* variously called it a case of 'Google Executive Hugo Barra [being] poached by China's Xiaomi'.[9] Barra's exit did not escape the attention of tabloids either. His resignation came in literally a few hours after the news broke that his former girlfriend and senior Google employee, Amanda Rosenberg, was dating Google founder Sergey Brin. The magazine *Vanity Fair* speculated that in light of current developments, Barra's hasty move was hardly a matter of coincidence.[10]

Barra, of course, has never commented on the rumoured love triangle involving Rosenberg and Brin and whether that had any part to play in his surprise resignation, but he has on a few occasions mentioned that he was in regular contact with the folks at Xiaomi for years before he got an actual job offer. In an All Things Digital interview, Barra revealed that his association with the people at Xiaomi dated back to the time when he joined Google in London. He was reported as saying, 'We had teams all over, but every quarter we had this thing called the mobile leadership summit, where we did project reviews and strategy sessions … Coincidentally, on my second day at Google, I was on a plane flying to Beijing, where we were having that particular quarter's meeting.'[11] This was in 2008 and Xiaomi was not yet born. At the time, Lin Bin, who was going

---

9   https://www.bbc.com/news/technology-23879496; https://www.indiatimes. com/technology/enterprise/google-android-executive-hugo-barra-poached- by-chinas-smartphone-maker-xiaomi-98486.html; https://www.cnbc.com/ 2017/01/23/xiaomi-hugo-barra-leaving-silicon-valley-google.html

10   https://www.vanityfair.com/style/2014/04/sergey-brin-amanda- rosenberg-affair

11   http://allthingsd.com/20130912/exclusive-hugo-barra-talks-about-his- future-at-xiaomi-and-why-he-left-google/

to become a co-founder and president at Xiaomi two years later, was working for Google's mobile unit in China under veteran technologist Kai Fu Lee. Once Barra and Lin met, the two stayed in touch. Their close association quickly turned into a friendship founded on mutual respect. Bin, whose job it was to localize the Android operating system for the Chinese market, consulted Barra on Android-related matters. Later, when Bin joined Xiaomi, Barra could not help but marvel at the kind of work the small start-up was doing in Beijing. Barra started bringing Xiaomi devices from his Beijing trips to show off to colleagues at Google. When the Android design head, Matías Duarte, praised the work Xiaomi was doing in extending the Android platform, it was an important moment for Barra. 'Matías's opinion really mattered a lot, and it was a big signal they were doing something right, and a pretty significant vote of confidence,' he said.[12] For Barra, the validation was important when the time came to accept Xiaomi's offer. Moreover, 'it was a once-in-a-lifetime opportunity, truly a dream job, this idea of building a global company which could be as significant as Google, from the ground up,' Barra said. 'It was just something that I will never come across, with a team whom I know, with a company that has DNA similar to my own and, on top of that, to live in Asia for at least some period of time.'[13]

Whatever may have spurred Barra's surprising exit, what was evidently Google's loss was soon going to be Xiaomi's gain. Xiaomi's president Lin Bin and CEO Lei immediately took to

---

12 https://www.theguardian.com/technology/2013/sep/12/hugo-barra-google-xiaomi-mobile-android-software

13 https://www.slashgear.com/hugo-barra-talks-about-xiaomi-google-and-future-ambitions-12297627/

their personal Sina Weibo accounts (China's microblogging website, very similar to Twitter) to announce the 'exciting news' of Barra coming on board in October 2013. After completing a whole week at Xiaomi's Beijing office, Barra himself took to Twitter on 15 October 2013 to let his followers know that it had been a 'pretty intense journey so far'. He was not exaggerating; if flinging himself some 10,500km away from his comfort zone in Mountain View was not enough, Barra found himself facing one of the biggest challenges of his career as he gently took over the reins of a Chinese start-up that was still largely unknown in the world he had left behind.

For their part, the co-founders at Xiaomi were a lot more confident of the value Hugo Barra was going to bring to their start-up. His years at Google had made him a familiar face at Android product launches, but Barra's career graph showed that he had been dabbling in product management for a lot longer. Lei Jun, Lin Bin and the company's leadership were all big on product, and they hit it off pretty well from the start.

Barra was born in 1976 in Belo Horizonte in Brazil but later moved to the US to attend college. In 1996 as an undergrad at the elite MIT, which has a 7 per cent acceptance rate, twenty-year-old Barra was at once juggling courses in management, computer science and electrical engineering while simultaneously performing the role of senior class president.[14] When he returned to MIT in 2001 to complete his master's degree in electrical engineering, he founded a speech recognition company as part of MIT's media lab. Barra decided to name his first company Lobby7, perhaps to remind himself where it had all

14 https://thealumnisociety.com/hugo-barra/

started—at the seventh building by the lobby to MIT's famous Infinite Corridor. Lobby7 wasn't a big success, but Scansoft Inc., an acquisitive tech company, bought it in 2003.[15] Fresh out of college, Barra joined Scansoft as product manager along with seven others. He rose rapidly to the role of director in 2004. The next year, Scansoft merged with Nuance Communications, a pioneering speech recognition company, where Barra continued to serve as director until he stepped down in 2008. Even in his capacity as Nuance's director, however, Barra continued to research extensively on mobile voice search and voice messaging software. He even launched a number of speech recognition products under Nuance's brand name. Nuance, the makers of speech recognition software Dragon NaturallySpeaking, became one of the leading providers of voice recognition technologies.[16] Barra's direct engagement and leadership at Nuance did not go unnoticed.

Google, founded by Larry Page and Sergey Brin—PhD students at Stanford University in 1996, the year Barra joined college—had gone public in 2004. The fast-growing internet search company had acquired YouTube for $1.65 billion in 2006, DoubleClick for $3.1 billion in 2007 and was rapidly charting its course to become one of the world's most valuable tech companies. It was hoovering up talent from around the world to build massively scalable consumer internet products. In March 2008, Barra flew out to London to begin work at Google's UK headquarters as group product manager.

---

15 https://techpp.com/2017/01/23/hugo-barra-things-to-know/

16 https://www.theguardian.com/technology/2014/jun/17/voice-recognition-nuance-samsung; https://www.theguardian.com/money/2018/sep/22/voice-recognition-is-it-really-as-secure-as-it-sounds

Android, mobile internet and Xiaomi's foresight

No doubt Google offered a great platform for someone of Barra's calibre. Just four years from a successful IPO, Google was teeming with great talent from around the world and was hungry for more. By 2009, Barra was product management director of mobile at Google. By the end of 2010, having served nearly two and a half years at Google's London office as product management director (mobile), Barra returned to the US—this time joining the Google office in California as director of product management, Android. Barra was now a regular face at Android's product launches, delivering keynotes at Google I/O, the company's much-awaited annual developer conference, and doing demos at other Google events alongside Eric Schmidt and Andy Rubin.

The evolution of the mobile phone industry in the last five years had been so remarkable that Google started paying even closer attention to the mobile internet. In the summer of 2010, at a Google in-house presentation at Zurich, Google's business development manager Amanda Rosenberg revealed Google's research estimates: mobile internet would outpace desktop internet in merely two years.[17]

Later that year in November, Wall Street analyst Mary Meeker published a report titled 'Ten Questions Internet Execs Should Ask & Answer'. The report pointed out that mobile is 'ramping faster than any new thing', and asked, 'is your business leading or lagging?'[18] Mobile internet use in the

---

17 https://www.youtube.com/watch?v=MUQMtFMXx8I&t=6s
18 https://techcrunch.com/2010/11/16/ten-questions-internet-execs-should-ask-and-answer/

US had already touched 120 million subscribers in just three to four years since the launch of the iPhone. In comparison, desktop internet, which began its growth in the mid nineties, had seen a slower growth curve. She also made a remarkable observation at the time: Android and iOS were ramping up quickly, eating into the market share of Symbian, Blackberry and others. Moreover, smartphone shipments had overtaken PC shipments within two years, signalling a rapid 'land grab evolution of internet access'.

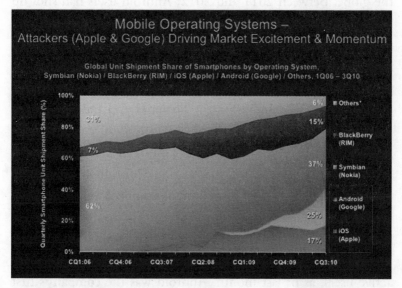

Source: Mary Meeker report, 2010.[19]

Mary Meeker's report may have been revelatory to many present in the room that day, but in the Chinese tech world, this was but old news. Xiaomi's founder Lei had hailed the 2010s as the

---

19 https://www.slideshare.net/marketingfacts/mary-meekers-internet-trends-2010

decade of the mobile internet way back in 2008. Speaking at UCWeb's strategy conference, Lei had exclaimed how 'mobile internet is becoming a trend'. If anything, what Google proposed as a future possibility was already part of the reality in markets such as China and Japan. The 2012 I/O offered further proof of Lei's foresight. Barra had become the vice president of Android by then. Pacing across the I/O stage in his signature black tee, Barra threw some staggering numbers at his audience.[20] The previous couple of years had seen a sharp rise in smartphone users across the globe. Between 2011 and 2012, Android users had shot up from 100 million to 400 million.[21] Google's internal research showed that close to 1 million Android devices were being activated daily. Markets in France, South Korea and Japan had grown by 200 to 300 per cent in one year. As for the developing countries—such as India, Brazil, Thailand and Indonesia—the markets for Android devices had grown by 500 per cent since 2011.[22] By 2015, Android was on 1.4 billion devices and by May 2019, a third of the world's population, 2.5 billion users, were on Android. As journalist Emil Protalinski noted in VentureBeat, 'That's more than the 1.5 billion PCs that Microsoft estimates are running Windows worldwide, a figure that hasn't been updated in years. It's also more than Facebook's 2.38 billion monthly active users, as of last month. Android was the company's first platform to reach the 2 billion mark.'[23] As emerging markets like India opened up to Android, and more and more people came to

---

20   https://www.youtube.com/watch?v=VuC0i4xTyrI&t=308s

21   Ibid.

22   Ibid.

23   https://venturebeat.com/2019/05/07/android-passes-2-5-billion-monthly-active-devices/

own smartphone devices for the first time, there was a lot to be excited about.

Barra's next big public interview happened in Paris at the LeWeb conference in 2013. By then, he had already quit Google, moved to Beijing and was busy promoting Xiaomi, discussing its product portfolios, and in general telling the world about how futuristic and astoundingly tech-driven the Chinese were. One could feel Barra's enthusiasm as he told his host (Loic Le Meur, founder at LeWeb) and audience members about his life since the big move to China.[24] This was a new role for him. Unlike his previous events at Google, which required no introduction and were entirely about new product launches, Xiaomi's international promotions were never solely about its devices. In his initial days, Barra was as much the brand ambassador for Chinese tech as he was the vice president of Xiaomi Global. Xiaomi, Barra would often be heard saying, was certainly a forerunner changing the tech scene in China, but he would never fail to mention the other stars in the Chinese constellation—Baidu, Alibaba, Tencent—who too were doing excellent work to bring superior technology into the hands of their consumers. This had always been Lei's dream—to transform the world's opinion about China by building an ecosystem so that people could see China for what it had become—a country that is responsible for bringing cutting-edge technological innovation to the world. Using ex-Googler Hugo Barra as the new face of Xiaomi gave credibility to that narrative.

Barra was revered by tech bloggers. ' ... we lost count of the number of people who wanted to get their pictures clicked with

---

24 https://www.youtube.com/watch?v=mZsvJUa9FpI&t=771s

the charismatic Xiaomi Vice President', tech journalist Nimish Dubey wrote in 2014 after attending an event in Delhi where Xiaomi unveiled a new phone.[25] Dubey, who called Barra Xiaomi's 'secret weapon', pointed out:

> 'Hugo Barra, unlike a lot of senior executives we have seen in the world of technology, does not talk DOWN to an audience. He talks to it. We saw proof of this again and again at Delhi last week when he often himself carried the microphone to questioners during the Q&A session and on a couple of occasions, Hugo Barra even sat down right next to them while answering the questions.'

Employees who worked at Xiaomi concur. 'He was a no bullshit guy. If you had an idea, no matter how low on the ladder you are, you could take it to him,' said a former employee on condition of anonymity. The same can't be said for executives at most Chinese companies that tend to be hierarchical.

Sceptics still preferred calling Xiaomi 'the Apple of China', but thanks to Barra, for most others, it now stood for a young, fast-growing company that was ready to take on the global market. Until then, Xiaomi had been a prosperous Chinese company, and there were many of those, including old rivals such as Meizu. The name Xiaomi, which literally means millet, also alluded to the Communist Party of China's use of the 'millet and rifle' symbol during the historic Second Sino-Japanese War of 1937–45. Xiaomi may have been a twenty-first-century tech company, but in spirit, it shared some of Chinese revolutionary

---

25 https://techpp.com/2014/09/05/hugo-barra-profile-xiaomi/

history. This is a common trait seen in many Chinese private enterprises, including Huawei and Alibaba. It was fine so long as Xiaomi continued operations in China. But as an aspiring brand with global ambitions, Xiaomi had to go easy on communist symbolism, albeit it being weak. In other words, it had to strike a balance between portraying itself as a loyal Chinese company and a cool tech company. In September 2013, a month before Barra officially came on board, the Singapore-headquartered blog *Tech in Asia* ran a report asking if Xiaomi had redacted the communist red star from its mascot. Xiaomi's mascot was a bunny with a red five-pointed star on its furry hat or ushanka, a headgear worn typically by communist rebels. In September, *Tech in Asia* noted that Xiaomi's Facebook fan page in Taiwan had removed the red star from its mascot's hat. The red star itself was not problematic—renowned global brands such as Heineken and Macy's use it—but as the report rightly pointed out, 'the ubiquity of the red star doesn't erase its political connotations, especially when it's on an Ushanka. And even if the red star itself has been depoliticized in China, that doesn't necessarily apply outside of the country's borders.'[26] It was clear that Xiaomi was taking the issue of its global rebranding rather seriously. These little changes have had ripple effects on Xiaomi's brand perception years later.

The company had started making news outside China ever since Barra had come in as a significant hire. It was now time to make some serious moves. But the name itself proved to be a source of confusion among non-Chinese users. For those who are unfamiliar, it was hard to pronounce. Thus, in 2014,

---

26 https://www.techinasia.com/xiaomi-redacted-communist-red-star-mascot

Xiaomi's founders decided to shorten its name to Mi as a way to increase brand awareness and facilitate ease of brand recall among its international patrons. Mi, they said, was shorthand for mobile internet. In April 2014, Xiaomi purchased the internet domain called mi.com for $3.6 million, purportedly the most expensive domain ever bought in China.[27] Apart from being an abbreviation for mobile internet, Xiaomi's home page mentioned that Mi additionally stood for 'mission impossible', 'because Xiaomi faced many challenges that had seemed impossible to defy in our early days'. Mi was an easy name to remember, had potential brand recall value and was sure to find great traction among new users. 'The advantage was that mi.com was appropriate to international promotion—this domain name made it much easier to spread the concept of "mobile internet" on a global basis,' Li Wanqiang, co-founder and chief brand officer of Xiaomi, wrote in his 2016 book *The Xiaomi Way: Customer Engagement Strategies That Built One of the Largest Smartphone Companies in the World.*[28] Now, Xiaomi was ready for the global market.

Singapore becomes Xiaomi's first international beachhead

Six months after appointing Hugo Barra and a little before it shortened its name to Mi, in February 2014, the company made its first official launch outside Greater China (which includes

---

27 https://www.cnet.com/news/xiaomi-spent-3-6m-on-new-two-letter-domain/

28 Li Wanqiang, *The Xiaomi Way: Customer Engagement Strategies that Built One of the Largest Smartphone Companies in the World.* New York: McGraw-Hill Education, 2016.

Mainland China, Hong Kong and Taiwan). Following in the tradition of most Chinese tech that had come before it, Singapore was chosen as Xiaomi's first international testing ground before it continued on its path along the rest of Southeast Asia and India. On 21 February 2014, Xiaomi devices went on sale in Singapore, the island state with over 85 per cent smartphone penetration with about 5 million inhabitants. The launch was attended by Lin Bin and Hugo Barra. Speaking of the scale of the launch, Barra said,

> 'The initial roll-out efforts in these countries will be slow and small only because we want to make sure we are doing the right things. There are all sorts of carrier-related issues that we sometimes can't really get right the first time around. So we're going to start small then ramp up as quickly as the market wants us to ramp up, in Malaysia and beyond.'[29]

Xiaomi's first international entry was successful, although Singapore, being a small country, did not influence the company's global rankings. With booming sales in China, by the third quarter of 2014, it had outpaced many other global brands to emerge as the world's fifth-largest smartphone manufacturer. By 2015, it started inching closer to the top in global rankings. Xiaomi shipped more than 17 million smartphones or 5.3 per cent out of 327.8 million smartphones shipped worldwide, according to IDC. Samsung led the rankings in the same period with a total

---

29   https://www.zdnet.com/article/xiaomi-kicks-off-global-expansion-with-singapore-launch/

of 78.1 million shipments, followed by Apple at 39.3 million. Lenovo and LG were neck and neck, with just under 17 million smartphones shipped in the same period. This is the first time Xiaomi broke into the top three global rankings. But it was only the beginning. Keeping to his old blogging habits, Lei posted his initial reactions following Xiaomi's remarkable global ranking. It hinted at Lei's limitless ambition. He wrote,

> 'A Chinese company, sitting in the world's largest consumer market, has achieved internal business results under the advantage of local operations, and it is probably very satisfying. But we haven't positioned ourselves only in the Chinese market, because the journey we yearn for is still broader ... The future battlefield will be global. This year, we accidentally had the opportunity to enter the top five in the world. In the future, we will show the world the power of science and technology innovation from China.'[30]

For Lei, Xiaomi's achievements were merely 'accidental'. Lei, a realist who liked to say that if everything came together, even 'pigs can fly', knew that companies were naturally designed to fail at least a few times in their life cycle, and any great accomplishment was often closely followed by greater challenges. Lei's speculations were not wholly unfounded. Many had pointed out that Xiaomi was destined to run into patent disputes once it left the Chinese mainland, where intellectual property (IP) rights were comparatively lax. Moreover, penetrating more mature markets

---

30 Lei Jun's blog.

such as the US, UK and Europe would require a different set of strategies since Xiaomi's potential consumers in developed countries were most likely looking for replacements for their existing devices and were not first-time smartphone users like the majority of the population out in south and Southeast Asia. The threat of China's worsening trade relations with the US and tensions with India was not on its radar yet. For now, however, Xiaomi was happy riding the wave of its initial overseas success and bracing itself to enter India.

In July 2014, Xiaomi launched in India—a country of over 1 billion people with an economy growing at a healthy clip. India was more than 200 times the size of Singapore by population but smartphone penetration of less than 10 per cent. This time too, it followed the same method as the Singapore launch, starting small and releasing a few thousand phones at a time. At this point, Xiaomi was exclusively available via online sales and word-of-mouth promotions. Its first flash sale on home-grown e-commerce website Flipkart was a massive success, and all the units were sold out in five seconds (more on this in Chapter 4).

As Xiaomi grew a year older, operations also became more and more elaborate. Lei no longer had enough time to write regular blog entries as he had done even a few years ago. But, at the turn of 2015, he returned to his personal blog to wish his followers a prosperous new year adding,

'2014 is bound to become an important milestone in the development history of Xiaomi: we have changed from a chaser in the industry to an object chased by the entire industry. Even at the end of the year, we encountered patent lawsuits from international giants and welcomed Xiaomi's ritual of maturity.'

Clearly, from a year of 'accidental' accomplishments, Xiaomi was now slowly transitioning into a period of maturity.

As news of crazy flash sales continued to pour in from all quarters, Hugo Barra's alma mater MIT acknowledged Xiaomi's tech leadership. In 2015, *MIT Technology Review*'s prestigious list of fifty smartest companies ranked Xiaomi second, following only behind Tesla Motors, leaving tech giants such as Apple, Google, Uber and even Chinese giants Baidu and Tencent trailing.[31] Coming from a well-respected Western publication, this was a big win for Xiaomi. Not merely because Xiaomi beat industry heavyweights by such a large margin but mostly because it had leapfrogged from its 2014 ranking of number thirty in such an unprecedented way.[32] For a company that was unknown to the world outside China until mid 2013, whose name was obscure and so hard to pronounce that critics preferred to call it the Apple of China, emerging as the second-best smart company by 2015 was an incredible feat. It was also the kind of international validation that made Xiaomi's global expansion a lot easier after 2015.

As part of his new year's resolution for 2015, Lei wrote on his blog the following lines:

31 https://www.technologyreview.com/lists-tr50/50-smartest-companies-2015/

32 https://www.technologyreview.com/lists-tr50/50-smartest-companies-2014/

'Go to the world with dreams. We have gone abroad and entered 7 countries and regions overseas, with great success there. We have sold more than 1 million mobile phones in the Indian market. This year we will enter more overseas markets, and we will face more new challenges in internationalization. The road to success has never been smooth. We will overcome obstacles, ride the wind and waves, and bring high-quality technology products from China to all places where the sun can shine. We want to make technology fun for everyone around the world!'

In the five years following its launch, Xiaomi would go on to sell 100 million phones in India and quickly become a challenger brand in evolved markets such as Spain, France and Italy.[33]

In 2015, Xiaomi launched in Brazil, a country with a population of over 200 million. In some ways, the Brazil launch also signalled a full circle for Barra, who had left the South American country as a teenager to attend college in the US, only to return to his homeland almost two decades later for the much-anticipated Xiaomi launch. 'We already had a very engaged community of Mi fans in Brazil before our launch today, and many of them have been eagerly looking forward to getting their hands on our products,' Barra told journalists during the event. The hype created by Xiaomi fans (Mi Fans who play an important role in Xiaomi's growth) just before a big launch was practically a tradition by now. Given Xiaomi's popularity both at home and abroad (in the few countries it had already entered), tech

---

33 https://www.livemint.com/technology/tech-news/xiaomi-sells-100-
    million-smartphones-in-india-1567756450092.html

amateurs and experts alike across the world had begun to take notice of the Chinese start-up's ability to churn out high-specs smartphones. Like in India, so in Brazil, there was a substantial fan base even before the devices had entered its domestic market.

Admiration in the US, but entry tough

Out in the US, tech journalists were awestruck by how quickly Chinese tech products had taken over the Western market. In a 2015 feature stereotypically titled 'Enter the Dragon', *Fortune* magazine did a profile on Chinese start-ups such as OnePlus, Oppo and Xiaomi that had entered the global tech scene, remarking how, back in 2012, 'China passed the US as the world's largest smartphone market. Since then, its number of annual phone shipments, has doubled, to about 400 million—enough for every man, woman, and child in the US and Canada with tens of millions to spare.'[34] The Chinese wave was not a particularly unique phenomenon—the seventies had witnessed a similar Japanese wave as brands such as Sony, Sanyo and Sharp flooded the Western market. This was followed by the South Korean deluge around the noughties as Samsung, Hyundai and LG 'repeated the exercise on their Japanese forerunners: undercut on price, outpace with innovation, profit'. The mid 2010s, *Fortune* observed, was evidently the 'Chinese era'. 'We are now facing a new era in consumer electronics, a Chinese era, studded with a new generation of wily entrepreneurs and clever engineers armed with lessons learned from those that came before.'[35] Responding

---

34 https://fortune.com/longform/china-smartphone-domination/
35 Ibid.

to what *Fortune* was now describing as the great Chinese wave, Richard Liu, director of Morningside Venture Capital, a friend of Lei Jun and one of Xiaomi's earliest investors, clarified, 'This is probably just the beginning of the wave.'[36]

At the Code Conference in 2015, Barra talked about global expansion into the US and Europe. At the time of the conference, Xiaomi had already created a huge market base not only in Mainland China but also in Greater China, which includes Taiwan and Hong Kong. It had also penetrated markets in Singapore, Malaysia, India and Indonesia. With Brazil's launch successfully completed, Xiaomi was now looking to capture markets in the UK, Germany, France and even the US in order to sell Xiaomi accessories. Xiaomi had by then started producing a broad range of tech accessories, which included wearables such as the Mi Band (with a fitness and sleep tracker), high-end headphones, power bank chargers and even selfie sticks. As a way to increase the fanfare around Xiaomi's products, from June 2015, the official Mi website allowed customers in Europe and the US to buy these accessories, even though actual phones were still unavailable in these locations.

Entering the US market had always been a strong consideration for Xiaomi, but in 2015, it was not yet a realistic expansion strategy. Having worked in the Google ecosystem for over five years, Barra, of course, had a keener sense of how things worked out there. At the 2015 Code Conference, he explained why the US was such a different market from what Xiaomi had already encountered during its overseas expansion. 'It is such a competitive market,' Barra said while explaining the existing American market

---

36 Ibid.

conditions, 'It's not a price sensitive market, and not just because of its higher per capita than most developing nations, but because its carrier sensitivity model washes away a lot of price advantages that we have ... we would have to sell through operators.'[37] Barra was right. Even today, smartphones in the US are rarely sold directly and often come with 'monthly tab plans' with an existing telecom carrier. Working with carriers is an extremely time- and capital-intensive process. This meant Xiaomi's strategy of selling directly and exclusively through online flash sales would not work in the US. Moreover, Xiaomi would have to set up a strong network of after-sales service stations, which would need trained back-office executives. 'We have to enter the US with a spotless customer service,' Barra said. Given the logistics, a successful US launch was going to take years. Meanwhile, India emerged as Xiaomi's second-largest market after Greater China, after just about a year of being in business. This new development indicated that as vice president of Xiaomi Global, Barra's trips to India were to become more and more frequent. In fact, he was already spending so much time in Xiaomi India's Bengaluru office that he would often joke that it had become his 'second home'. There is little doubt that Xiaomi's tremendous success in India was a huge boost to the company and a greater validation of Barra's abilities as the company's vice president, but it also meant that Barra could not draw out an elaborate road map for the US expansion just yet; as he tiredly observed, 'I can't be in Bengaluru and San Francisco at the same time.'

Understandably, Barra and other senior associates at Xiaomi including Lin Bin and Lei Jun took time to slowly build relations

---

37 https://www.youtube.com/watch?v=sjA_nkHlq_k&t=1239s

in India and fortify Xiaomi's position as the number one brand in the country. But in the time that India became Xiaomi's second-largest market after Greater China, America's revised diplomatic and trade policies made Xiaomi's entry more improbable than ever. In November 2016, amidst despair and jubilation, Donald Trump was elected the new president of the US, at the end of President Barack Obama's term of eight long years. This was bad news for China, and more specifically for Xiaomi's future US plans. Trump's hatred for China was by then a widely known fact because even as a presidential candidate, he had not only been extremely vocal about China's unfair trade practices, but had even promised to impose huge tariffs and drastically restrict the import of Chinese products into the US if he was sworn in as the next president. Trump's initial tariff proposal, in fact, came in 2012 when he had first considered running for president. 'They [the Chinese] have manipulated their currency so violently towards this country, it is almost impossible for our companies to compete with Chinese companies,' Trump had told CNN back then, adding that he thought it necessary for the US government to levy a 25 per cent tariff on Chinese products.[38] In the face of an impending trade war between the US and China following Trump's appointment to office, Xiaomi's plans to enter the US market seemed more distant than ever before.

In January 2017, as Donald Trump prepared to assume office as the forty-fifth president of the US, Barra announced that he was stepping down as the vice president of Xiaomi Global after having served the company for three and a half years. In

38 https://money.cnn.com/2011/04/17/news/economy/trump_china_trade_war/index.htm

these years, Barra, who was touching forty, had spent most of his waking hours working, and he had aged visibly. A gnawing sense of homesickness was also starting to creep up on him. 'At Xiaomi, Hugo was always working and paid close attention to details. He's obsessed like that. But he also missed the social life back home and also the intense scrutiny that came with being Xiaomi's global face and a near celebrity was getting to him,' said a former Xiaomi employee who has worked closely with Barra.

On 22 January 2017, Barra wrote a post on Facebook discussing why he was quitting Xiaomi. He said, 'What I've realized is that the last few years of living in such a singular environment have taken a huge toll on my life and started affecting my health. My friends, what I consider to be my home, and my life are back in Silicon Valley, which is also much closer to my family. Seeing how much I've left behind these past few years, it is clear to me that the time has come to return.' Xiaomi's president and Barra's long-time friend Lin Bin too wrote a heartfelt note on Facebook, confirming Barra's departure. Bin said,

> 'When Hugo joined us 3 ½ years ago, we started an amazing adventure to turn Xiaomi into a global player. We have come a long way since, and I couldn't thank him enough for contributing so much to Xiaomi's journey. As much as we would love to have Hugo stay with us in Beijing for a much longer time, we understand his personal challenges and wish him all the best in his future endeavors.'

Indeed, Hugo had achieved a lot during his tenure as vice president of Xiaomi Global. Under Barra's leadership, India

had emerged as Xiaomi's largest international market, raking
in $1 billion in revenue for the first time in 2016—faster than
any company in India's history. At the time, Xiaomi had also
successfully expanded to twenty countries, including Indonesia,
Singapore, Malaysia and Poland, but India truly represented the
crowning glory of Barra's term as vice president. 'He actually
fought for a lot of autonomy for the Indian business because he
believed that was the only way to succeed,' the former Xiaomi
employee recalled. Until then, most Chinese companies operated
businesses in other countries with satellite offices and never truly
empowered these offices. In the case of Xiaomi, Barra changed
that, setting up the India team for success in the future.

As the tension between US and China escalated over the years
and Xiaomi's much-anticipated US expansion hit an impasse,
it seemed like the perfect occasion for Barra to move on. In
fact, only three days after Barra's resignation, Mark Zuckerberg
announced that Barra was joining Facebook. A day later, Barra
himself announced on Twitter that he was joining Facebook as
vice president of virtual reality.

> 'It's been a dream of mine to work in virtual reality even
> back when AR/VR were just figments of science fiction;
> now we're taking selfies in virtual worlds ☺ I learned
> from Xiaomi CEO Lei Jun that there's no greater calling in
> our industry than taking breakthrough tech and making
> it available to the greatest number of people.'

Doubtless, Barra's resignation left a gaping void in Xiaomi's global
expansion mission. But the show, as they say, went on. Manu
Jain, who until then had been the head of operations at Xiaomi

India, was appointed the new vice president of Xiaomi with the mandate of overseeing the company's business in South Asia. Global operations were transitioned over to Senior Vice President Wang Xiang, former President of Qualcomm China and one of the co-founders of Xiaomi. Entering the US market was still no more than a distant dream, but by May 2017, barely a few months after Hugo Barra had left the establishment, the Chinese start-up was on its way to announcing its Mexico launch. Many dubbed this launch as a case of Xiaomi 'sneaking into North America', with plans of entering the US by 2019. Xiaomi devices were not new to Mexico, having been previously made available via partners, but the launch marked a deeper penetration into the Mexican market. 'If nothing else,' TechCrunch suggested, 'Mexico isn't all that far away if Xiaomi fans in the US fancy a trip to pick up a device.'[39]

In many ways, 2017 marked an extraordinary year for Xiaomi. Having faced a setback in 2016 on account of poor sales, 2017 was the year of a great comeback. In a heartfelt letter addressed to all of Xiaomi's employees at the year-end gala, Lei Jun wrote,

> 'In October 2017, we exceeded the revenue goal of RMB 100 billion set at the beginning of the year. I checked—and found out that to achieve this milestone, Apple took 20 years, Facebook took 12 years, Google took nine years, Alibaba took 17 years, Tencent took 17 years, Huawei took 21 years ... Xiaomi has taken only slightly over seven years. We are very likely to

---

39 https://techcrunch.com/2017/05/09/xiaomi-mexico/

enter the Fortune Global 500 list of companies this year ... We have entered more than 70 markets globally and established a leading position in many of them. But this is just a start. There is still a lot of room for growth in the markets we are present in, and we have yet to enter many more markets around the globe. Overseas markets represent huge opportunities for us, and we need to give more support in terms of strategy, resources and localized product development, as well as send more of our employees out to the rest of the world ... In 2018, the Chinese smartphone market is poised to experience a decline for the first time after more than a decade of growth. The market is consolidating while the competition becomes more and more brutal. There is no turning back for us, and we have to charge forward. The Chinese market is Xiaomi's foundation. It is the biggest consumer electronics market in the world and the most competitive one. Only by winning in the domestic market can we have enough support for global expansion. Only by winning in China can we win in the rest of the world ... So, this year I am setting a new goal: We will regain the #1 position in China within 10 quarters.'

With telecommunications giant Huawei turning up the heat in the domestic market, becoming number one in China would prove harder for Xiaomi than Lei had anticipated. Between 2017 and 2019, Xiaomi ceded ground to the competition. But it finally entered the Fortune 500 global list in 2019, a year later than Lei had expected but even as such, and it was a tremendous

achievement: Xiaomi was the youngest debutant on the list.[40]
The year 2018 saw Xiaomi returning to its roots to fortify its
domestic market where its performance had suffered after it went
international. While Xiaomi devoted time and energy to new
markets, back home, Chinese smartphone companies such as
Huawei, OnePlus, Oppo and Vivo were slowly taking over the
prime position that Xiaomi had enjoyed even a couple of years
before. The battle of the Chinese brands had begun all over again.

Xiaomi goes public

Xiaomi's public listing was yet another important milestone in its
decade-long existence. It listed its IPO on the HKSE on 9 July
2018.

Xiaomi started venturing overseas in early 2014 following
the appointment of Hugo Barra as the global vice president. In
2015 the company reported losses, and by 2016 it had ceded
some market share to competitors in China. Many attribute this
slump to Xiaomi's hasty decision to move into the global market,
rendering it vulnerable to the competition back home from
companies such as Huawei, Oppo, Vivo and OnePlus.

However, Lei vowed to take the market back and turned
things around for the company. In 2017 it grew even bigger,
even though the competition was fierce. 'No firm had ever come
back from a wound that severe in the trench warfare of the global
smartphone business,' David Kline wrote in *Wired* magazine in

---

40 https://brandequity.economictimes.indiatimes.com/news/business-of-
    brands/xiaomi-becomes-youngest-company-on-fortune-global-500-
    list/70329834

December 2017.[41] Xiaomi dug itself out of the hole by launching a new phone, the Mi Mix 2, touted as the world's first bezel-less phone, selling offline at retail stores, and by aggressively pursuing its ecosystem strategy. It also grew by selling more phones in India. The gamble paid off.

In the days preceding Xiaomi's public listing, Lei wrote on the Mi blog about the company's various achievements in the past year,

'The numbers speak for themselves,'

He added:

'In 2017, we achieved annual revenues of 114.6 billion RMB, with 67.5% year-over-year growth. It only took us 7 years to cross this major milestone of 100 billion RMB. In Q1 2018, we achieved over 85.7% year-over-year growth, with our e-commerce and new retail platforms accounting for 63.7% of revenue. Last year, our internet services accounted for 8.6% of revenue, reaching an astonishing number of 9.9 billion RMB, while our Q1 2018 internet service revenue increased to 9.4% of revenue. This fully validates our ability to monetize internet services, proving that we can convert the traffic generated by our hardware and e-commerce channels into revenue and profit.'[42]

---

41 https://www.wired.com/story/behind-the-fall-and-rise-of-china-xiaomi/
42 http://blog.mi.com/en/2018/07/08/tomorrow-let-us-witness-a-great-milestone-together/

Written as an open letter to the company's fans and admirers, the blog post also doubled as a smart pitch for potential investors who were still on the fence about Xiaomi's credibility in the stock market.

Not surprisingly, the news of Xiaomi's imminent public listing had created ripples in the market although it wasn't quite clear yet if Xiaomi would list in the NYSE or the HKSE. The year 2018 marked the eighth year of Chinese company IPOs in the US. *Forbes* reported, 'Four of the top US IPOs in 2018 were from China: online video platform iQiyi at $2.4 billion on Nasdaq, social commerce upstart Pinduoduo at $1.7 billion on Nasdaq, electric car maker NIO at $1.2 billion on the New York Stock Exchange (NYSE), and Tencent Music at $1.1 billion on the NYSE.'[43] But what was perhaps the biggest public listing in tech history was Alibaba's mega $25 billion IPO in the NYSE in 2014.

Xiaomi, which had initially planned to raise $10 billion at a $100 billion valuation, was this big news story that could perhaps only be compared to Alibaba's stupendous IPO success in 2014. Given its staggering estimates, Xiaomi could easily become the third-biggest IPO in tech history after Alibaba (with a $167 billion valuation) and Facebook (with a $104 billion valuation). This was not just a huge success for Xiaomi, and even as speculations were rife regarding how much of this would actually be realized at the IPO, this also set an example of how China was aggressively challenging the US in matters of

---

43 https://www.forbes.com/sites/rebeccafannin/2019/09/29/a-ban-on-chinese-ipos-in-the-u-s-could-backfire-and-strengthen-chinas-resolve-to-get-ahead/#7642021f77ef

technological prowess and economic growth. China had already opened up its market following the great revolution, but with its growing ambition, Chinese firms were now setting out overseas to raise more capital. Few would have imagined that companies from communist China would vie for what Karl Marx once called 'fictitious capital'. In 2017 itself, as many as 137 Chinese companies had reportedly listed either in the US or in the Hong Kong market, including giants such as Foxconn, China Literature Ltd and Sogou Inc.

The NYSE had recently become a preferred destination for Chinese tech IPOs. New York offered higher valuations, a large pool of tech investors and had the reputation of being the world's biggest market. Meanwhile, the HKSE was also luring Chinese tech companies and its familiarity and close proximity to China and convenient time zone were top draws. Xiaomi's decision to go with the HKSE may have been driven by a familiarity of the Hong Kong market, but in hindsight, it was a practical move to shield itself from the ongoing US–China trade war that had been exacerbated since Donald Trump's appointment as president of the US in 2016. Days before it went public, the *Financial Times* predicted that if Xiaomi managed to realize its estimated figure, it would be the sixth-largest company in the HKSE. In its ten-year existence, Xiaomi had shown an uncanny ability to gauge the market. Its decision to go public at the HKSE once again proved how prophetic it was in its market intelligence. A year after Xiaomi went public, *Forbes* carried a report speculating what a possible and imminent ban on Chinese IPOs in the US could mean for both countries. The US–China trade war has only intensified over the years, and the news of the IPO ban came closely on the heels of the US declaring a ban on Huawei products in the US. In September 2019, *Forbes* reported,

> 'If a ban on Chinese listings in the US does occur, the Hong Kong Stock Exchange would be a primary beneficiary. The HKSE already has been a draw for going public. Last year (2018), 44 Chinese companies went public in Hong Kong and attracted $32 billion, nearly triple the level a year earlier.'[44]

It further stated, 'A recently opened Nasdaq-styled exchange in Shanghai could also pick up more listings from Chinese companies if a ban does become a reality. What a block could do is strengthen China's resolve to become the world's technology leader and to become more reliant on its own resources.'[45] Xiaomi's decision to list in the Hong Kong market proved once again that it was carefully weighing its options in the midst of this trade war and securing its future market prospects.

The news of Xiaomi's IPO proved once again that the Chinese giant was here to change the rules of the game. The *Economist*, in its Schumpeter column (named after famous economist Joseph Schumpeter, known for his theories in finance capitalism), said: 'Schumpeter's answer is that Xiaomi does not resemble any rich-world firm. For decades a particular American ideal of the public company has dominated: focused, widely owned and predictable. Xiaomi is a supercharged champion of a new Chinese model that is the opposite: deliberately sprawling, tightly controlled and

---

44 Ibid.
45 Ibid.

hyperactive.'[46] That the concept of entrepreneurship differed among Chinese and American firms was best exemplified in the reactions of their respective CEOs after Alibaba and Facebook went public. Addressing a technology conference sixteen months after Facebook's IPO, Mark Zuckerberg told his audience that the IPO had made Facebook a 'stronger company'. In contrast, CEO Jack Ma's reaction to Alibaba's jubilant IPO success was rather modest. Moments after the listing, Ma humbly stated, 'What we raised today is not money, it's the trust. It's the responsibilities that we have.'[47] Evidently, Lei Jun's mindset in the final hours before Xiaomi's listing was very similar to Jack Ma's. On the night before the listing (8 June 2018), Lei wrote an evocative letter to all the fans, employees, investors and loyalists who had supported Xiaomi along the way for eight long years. Lei wrote,

> 'I believe that Xiaomi's story will inspire and encourage even more entrepreneurs. When people evaluate Xiaomi 100 years from now, I hope that their perception is that the most important value from Xiaomi is not how many devices we sell or how much profit we make. Rather, I hope they see our value in changing people's lives and exploring new ways of doing business, including being friends with our users and making sure that our business goals are fully aligned with those of our users. We have proved that we can be successful if we have the courage to relentlessly innovate, diligently persevere, and be generous

---

46 https://www.economist.com/business/2018/06/07/xiaomis-forthcoming-ipo-shows-how-the-rules-of-business-are-changing

47 https://www.nyse.com/network/article/Alibaba-Lists-on-the-NYSE

and steadfast in our values ... The world will ultimately reward people who are diligent and generous. Tomorrow, Xiaomi will be a public company, but this is just a new beginning in our journey, and a public listing has never been our ultimate goal. We work tirelessly not because we want to become a public company. Instead, we have become a public company because it allows us to strive more to achieve our mission. A successful listing is only the first chapter of Xiaomi's story, and the second chapter will be even more splendid and dazzling.'[48]

Xiaomi's IPO did not, however, go as expected. It had initially estimated to sell shares in the price range of HK$17 to HK$22 per share. In the end, Xiaomi sold about 2.18 billion shares at HK$17 each ($2.17), scraping the bottom of the proposed price range. In all, Xiaomi raised $4.72 billion on a valuation of $54 billion making it the world's biggest tech float in four years since Alibaba's IPO in 2014. Critics dubbed it a 'reality check' on the company in what was easily the year's most closely watched IPO. While the Hong Kong listing, time difference and escalating tension between US and China made it increasingly difficult to generate interest among international investors, the IPO also exposed some of Xiaomi's own shortcomings. Xiaomi was the first company to apply for a Chinese Depository Receipt (CDR) before its IPO. Similar to the American Depository Receipts available in the US, the Chinese Regulatory Commission had started insisting that Chinese firms that were being listed outside

---

48 http://blog.mi.com/en/2018/07/08/tomorrow-let-us-witness-a-great-milestone-together/

of Mainland China also open a second listing in the domestic market through the issuance of CDRs. The CDR was meant to allow the company to raise money even from the domestic market. However, just before the IPO, Xiaomi decided to indefinitely postpone its CDR application until the Hong Kong listing had been completed, which meant that the additional capital that could have been raised from domestic investors was now zero.[49] Xiaomi, however, did not offer any concrete reason behind this sudden decision, only revealing that it would choose 'an appropriate opportunity' to issue CDRs in the near future. Besides, Xiaomi's stock performance was, according to many, average at best, and the overall negative investor sentiment in global equities was a possible reason for Xiaomi's underwhelming performance. One of the harshest criticisms perhaps came from Dickie Wong, executive director for research at Kingston Financial in Hong Kong. 'Honestly, Xiaomi is not an internet company … It's just a hardware company. That's the problem,' Wong was reported saying.[50] On top of that, Xiaomi had vowed to cap profits from smartphone sales at just 5 per cent. What critics failed to see is the future of Xiaomi as an internet company and the clever route it took to become that. By selling hardware at thin margins, Xiaomi was getting into the hands of millions of users. Typically, internet companies incur a cost to acquire new customers. In Xiaomi's case, the customer acquisition cost is negative. Meaning, if you look at Xiaomi as an internet company,

---

49 https://www.ft.com/content/3258b946-7390-11e8-b6ad-3823e4384287

50 https://www.cnbc.com/2018/07/05/xiaomi-faces-a-reality-check-in-its-closely-watched-ipo.html

instead of losing money to acquire new users, they were making money from them (more on this in chapter 5).

'Reality check' aside, the public listing also made many people very rich. In June 2018, Xiaomi's board of directors decided to reward Lei Jun $1.5 billion in stocks as a way to appreciate his contributions to the company. Later he donated this bonus to charity. The practice of awarding founders with generous stock packages prior to listings is not uncommon. CNBC reported, 'Tesla and JD.com both approved substantial stock-based compensation packages for their founders.'[51] Manu Jain, who reportedly holds 22.88 million shares in the company, gained close to ₹320 crore (~$42 million). Hugo Barra, who had left the company in 2017 to join Facebook, retained his stock options despite being a former employee. Barra, who was allotted 86 million shares, was estimated to gain about $209 million after the IPO. But the biggest gainers in this story were perhaps the first fifty-six employees who collectively raised $11 million to invest in the start-up back in 2010. A Bloomberg report uncovered the story of Li Weixing, who had formerly worked as an engineer at Microsoft. Li, who has since been identified as Xiaomi's employee number twelve, was one of the first people to show interest in investing in Xiaomi with the RMB 500,000 (roughly $79,000) he had saved up. Li realized that his savings were not enough to buy a house, and so he wanted to invest in the new start-up instead. Seeing Li's interest, Lei Jun decided that they couldn't simply let Weixing invest without allowing the rest of employees to pitch in with whatever little they could gather. Among the investors were

---

51 https://www.cnbc.com/2018/06/22/xiaomi-reportedly-awards-founder-
    1-point-5-billion-in-stock-ahead-of-ipo.html

other regular employees who borrowed money from parents and one receptionist (employee number fourteen) who staked her dowry worth 100,000 to 200,000 yuan ($16,000–$31,000) to invest in Xiaomi in its early days. These fifty-six early investors were the lucky millionaires in Xiaomi's IPO story.[52] Speaking on this, venture capitalist and Xiaomi investor Richard Liu said, 'Lei Jun is the founder. He could afford all the capital. But why did he share with everyone? He has a vision, and he can build up that strong belief, and people are willing to take the huge risks.'[53]

52 https://www.scmp.com/tech/article/2147184/lucky-56-xiaomi-ipo-make-dozens-workers-millionaires

53 https://economictimes.indiatimes.com/markets/ipos/fpos/xiaomis-ipo-will-make-dozens-of-lucky-workers-millionaires/articleshow/64790298.cms

4

The Rocketship and the Man from Meerut

I N LATE 2013, SENIOR officials at Xiaomi were drawing up a possible expansion strategy for the company. India was one name in the list of emerging markets that they wanted to enter. It's an open market with a population of over a billion people. And most of them are young. By 2018, the country was going to enter a thirty-seven-year period of demographic dividend, where the working-age population would be greater than the population of dependants. Though not as populous as China, India still had a huge demography that was yet to see high quality smartphones at affordable pricing. This was Xiaomi's big opportunity to get in and put Mi phones in the hands of as many Indians as possible. To be sure, India was no virgin market—South Korean consumer electronics giant Samsung had been selling smartphones in the country since 2007. Other brands of the MENS club (Motorola,

Ericsson and Nokia apart from Samsung) were also present in the market with feature phones as well as smartphones running on their own operating systems. Home-grown brands such as Micromax, Intex, Lava and Karbonn, or MILK, as the informal acronym goes, imported phones from China and had been in operation for quite some time. But Xiaomi reckoned it could still carve out a niche for itself, given India's status as an emerging market and its large population. That was the initial plan—to get a slice of that big pie that was India. In the years that followed, Xiaomi managed to carve out the biggest slice of that pie for itself—it not only became the biggest smartphone seller in India, but the country also emerged as the second-largest market for Xiaomi after China. The company became the number one seller of fitness bands and TV screens on the back of its low-price, high-spec offerings.

Xiaomi launched in India in July 2014. Though it was successful in China, it was an unknown brand in India. At the time, Gurgaon-based Micromax was the key home-grown player taking on Samsung, with other brands such as Nokia, Motorola, Lava and Karbonn fighting for the third spot. In all, there were over 300 brands selling phones in all sizes and shapes in India at the time.

Micromax, founded in 2000 by entrepreneurs Vikas Jain, Rahul Sharma, Sumeet Kumar and Rajesh Agarwal, started selling mobile phones in 2008. By 2014-15, it was sitting pretty with a revenue of nearly $2 billion, the backing of Sequoia Capital, and was India's biggest mobile phone company. It even managed to become India's top-selling brand by volume in the first half of 2014.

'Micromax, in a first, has overtaken mighty South Korean rival Samsung to become India's biggest handset player with a 17 percent share. What's more, the desi hustler has pipped Finnish giant Nokia to become the leading feature phone brand. Two other Indian players, Karbonn and Lava, are among the top five feature phone makers. Karbonn is also the third biggest smartphone brand during the quarter,'

The *Forbes India* report quoted above was based on the data of the first two quarters of 2014.[1] Samsung followed close with 14 per cent. Nokia, Karbonn and Lava were at 11 per cent, 9 per cent and 6 per cent, respectively. The rest made up the remaining 43 per cent. The second quarter reports also showed that feature phone sales were down by 16 per cent even as growth in smartphone sales were nearly touching 68 per cent. The great Indian smartphone migration had begun, and Xiaomi's entry couldn't have been timed better.

Xiaomi made a splash when it sold all of its inventory (10,000 devices) in just a few seconds on India's popular e-commerce site Flipkart. But it was nowhere close to being a serious competitor to other brands that had established a strong foothold in the Indian market over the course of several years. Besides, Xiaomi still had one more challenge that it had to urgently overcome before it could successfully penetrate this foreign market. Indians, like the rest of the world, harboured great scepticism towards the quality and brand value of Chinese products. Long ago, Xiaomi's CEO

---

1   https://www.forbesindia.com/article/my-learnings/holy-cow-milk-turns-sour/51049/1

Lei Jun had identified this scepticism of Made in China goods as a major stumbling block in Xiaomi's path to global expansion. In fact, he dreamt that some day Xiaomi would redeem China's reputation with superior products that were honestly priced. As Xiaomi entered India, his vision and strategy were immediately put to trial. The other significant international brand in the race was Samsung, but as a South Korean company, neither did it share Xiaomi's Chinese heritage nor its China tag. Besides, Samsung had already spent nearly eighteen years in India and was a household name by the time Xiaomi entered the country. Samsung had established its R&D department in Bengaluru way back in 1996; it began manufacturing refrigerators in India in 2003 and smartphones in 2007. In 2014, the Indian ecosystem was pretty full with Samsung sharing space with Nokia and Motorola, who were almost on their way out, and a handful of domestic Indian brands that were all thriving. Unlike in the West, Apple was never a big player in India because of the price-sensitive nature of the market. Breaking into this league was, of course, going to take great marketing genius, but first, Xiaomi had to reinstate India's faith in a Chinese brand.

If Indians distrusted a Chinese brand like Xiaomi, in its turn, Xiaomi too was apprehensive about letting its Indian employees run operations autonomously. The original plan, therefore, was to employ only five to ten people at the India office and let them monitor and push sales, while the Chinese offices would do the heavy-lifting with respect to products and take executive decisions. As the vice president of Xiaomi Global, Hugo Barra was, of course, in charge of overseeing a successful launch, but Xiaomi still needed someone else to head everyday operations in India. This was when Manu Jain, a rather unknown start-up

founder at the time, came into the picture. Jain, the first employee
of Xiaomi India, worked out of his apartment. He then moved
to a coffee shop and then a tiny six-seater office. In April 2018,
Xiaomi moved into a 180,000-square-foot plush office with over
750 seats in Bengaluru. If someone had asked him where the
business would be in ten years, his answer probably would have
been very off. Because no one could have predicted Xiaomi's
phenomenal success in India.

'It was a little embarrassing. People would come, and we'd
discuss deals worth ₹10 crore, and they'd ask, "Where's your
team?" And I'd say I'm the India head, and I'm the team. There's
nobody else. I would serve coffee. I would open the door, and I
would do everything,' Jain recalled of Xiaomi India's early days in
an interview with Anand Daniel, a venture capitalist with Accel
Partners.[2]

In many ways, Jain was an unusual choice to head a consumer
electronics company. At the time, mobile phone companies in
India were run by veterans such as Pradeep Jain, managing director
at Karbonn with over twenty years of experience in the telecom
sector, and Rahul Sharma, who co-founded Micromax in 2000.
Sharma, and fellow entrepreneurs Rajesh Agarwal, Sumeet Arora
and Vikas Jain, had started Micromax and had sold everything
ranging from IT peripherals to telecom equipment. It was serious
business and serious money. Compared with these men, Manu
Jain was a newbie who, because of his previous occupations, had
not closely participated in India's fast-evolving telecom industry

---

2   https://medium.com/accel-india-insights/insights-38-manu-kumar-jain-
    on-scaling-xiaomi-and-disrupting-the-indian-electronics-spacedraft-1-
    c50c330b5ed3

as it transitioned from landlines to feature phones to smartphones like Pradeep Jain or Sharma did.

Manu Jain, thirty-three at the time, had no experience in the telecom sector. But he had previously co-founded Jabong, another leading Indian e-commerce company like Flipkart, and was thus naturally privy to the knowledge, insights and idiosyncrasies of the country's emerging e-commerce market. Jain, the young man from Meerut who had an engineering degree from India's top college (IIT—Indian Institute of Technology—Delhi) and a management degree from the Indian Institute of Management (IIM) Calcutta, was just the person Xiaomi was looking for.

Jain was also a breath of fresh air in the otherwise uppity world of mobile phone company chiefs. Dubey of TechPP wrote in 2015: [3]

'Like Barra, he is very accessible. And exudes a charm of his own. One that is built around laughter. I remember talking to him about the Xiaomi controversy with the Indian Air Force [when the IAF had allegedly circulated a memo asking its staff not to use Xiaomi handsets] and what struck me most was the sangfroid of the man. He seemed unflappable. Not in a cold, efficient manner. But well, in a surprising warm one,'

Asked how they see Jain, a former employee said, 'If Barra, with his technical bent, is like Steve Jobs, Manu, for his business acumen is like Tim Cook.' For this book, I met with Jain once, around the month of November of 2019. He asked me several questions

---

3   https://techpp.com/2015/06/25/manu-kumar-jain-profile/

about publishing and promised to think about spending more time on interviews. But that never materialized, so this chapter has been pieced together from interviews with current and former employees as well as public sources of information.

Learnings at Jabong

Born into a family of traders, Jain grew up in Meerut, a thriving city that is about a couple of hours drive from India's capital New Delhi. Most of his family lived in the same region in a community of sorts set up by his great-grandfather. He calls himself a 'mediocre student', but that's him being humble. Getting into IIT and then IIM Calcutta is not something mediocre students usually accomplish, at least not in the traditional sense of accomplishment.

After graduating, he moved to Bengaluru to take up a job at a start-up called TechSpan in 2003. He quit the job after a couple of years to study management at IIM Calcutta. Here he met his future wife Minu and then joined McKinsey & Company upon finishing the course.

Jain took a plunge into the world of e-commerce with Jabong in 2011 after working as an engagement manager at the consulting firm McKinsey for five years. Jabong was an online lifestyle and fashion retail platform. It was Praveen Sinha, Manu's classmate from IIM Calcutta, who convinced him to join the Rocket Internet-backed Jabong as a co-founder. Indian start-ups were beginning to attract funding, talent and attention. But it was still an unlikely idea that people would buy fashion goods online, especially when it involved a lot of 'touch and feel'. But Sinha prevailed, and Manu became a co-founder.

In 2012, the *Economist* reported that Jabong had accomplished sales worth $100 million to $150 million.[4] This was an impressive figure for a company that had just entered India's fledgling e-commerce industry. Just three years ago, in 2009, the total e-commerce market in India was worth about $3.9 billion.[5] By 2011 it had increased to $6.3 billion, and in another year the market was estimated at $14 billion.[6] Clearly, Jabong had found a foothold within the now-thriving e-commerce industry. But in spite of the massive growth in e-commerce sales over just three years, the country was still predominantly anchored in offline sales. E-commerce was only about 2 per cent of the $650 billion-retail market then. The surge in online business was definitely a big development, and it got Jain seriously thinking about the prospect of internet businesses in India. He noticed that more than 60 to 70 per cent of Jabong's consumers were using their mobile phones—with two to three inch screens—to make online purchases. This was a big revelation since Jabong's online platform had been originally designed to work on desktop screens. Remember how Lei had predicted back in 2008 that the coming decade was going to be the age of the mobile internet? Well, in 2012, as Jain was going over the pattern of online engagement on Jabong's platform, he realized that the moment of the mobile internet had definitely arrived in India, but only a few had really seen it. 'That was my pivoting point,' Jain recalled later.

Mobile internet was taking off in India. Just about 71 million Indians claimed to have used the internet in 2009, and only

---

4   https://en.wikipedia.org/wiki/Jabong.com#cite_note-The_Economist-11

5   https://en.wikipedia.org/wiki/E-commerce_in_India

6   Ibid.

about 52 million of them were active users or used the internet at least once a month, as per a report by the Internet and Mobile Association of India. Mary Meeker, the foremost analyst on the state of the internet, in her 2012 report said that between 2008 and 2012 India had 88 million internet users, but by 2012 it grew by 26 per cent, reaching nearly 137 million people or about 11 per cent of the population.[7] Only China and the US were ahead of India by the number of internet users. At the time, India had only about 44 million smartphone subscribers making up about 4 per cent of the total mobile users in the country. This meant there was massive room for growth.

In 2013, Jain came across a Chinese blog that introduced him to Xiaomi. There were two things about the company that appealed to him immediately. First, while most other tech companies concentrated on either hardware or software, Xiaomi worked on both at the same time. The second aspect was perhaps even more compelling than the first—Xiaomi had until then spent no money towards marketing and sales promotions, relying instead on word-of-mouth publicity and online commerce almost exclusively. As an entrepreneur from India, where the new generation of venture-backed companies was spending millions of dollars on marketing, Xiaomi's maverick marketing philosophy surprised and intrigued Jain in equal measure. In the next few days, he got his friend and advisor Naveen Tewari, the founder of InMobi, to put him in touch with Xiaomi president Lin Bin. Tewari, like Jain, was an alumnus of the Indian Institute of Technology. He too had joined McKinsey afterwards even though they were never contemporaries. Rather, Tewari was

---

7   https://www.slideshare.net/kleinerperkins/2012-kpcb-internet-trends-yearend-update

like an elder brother to Jain, guiding him and mentoring him through his career. Founded in 2007, Tewari's company InMobi specialized in mobile advertising, putting him in close touch with leading phone makers across the world. InMobi was the first Indian company to raise megabucks from Softbank ($200 million in 2011), and Tewari was seen as a top entrepreneur.[8] Thanks to Tewari's great networking skills, Jain had no difficulty getting in touch with Xiaomi's Lin Bin. Unlike Lei Jun, Lin was comfortable communicating in English, and so over the next eighteen months, the two forged a strong relationship via email and phone calls, exchanging notes about the tech scene in India and China. By the end of 2013, Manu decided to leave Jabong and set off on a backpacking trip across China.

At the time, Jabong was doing good business and had already captured 25 per cent of the online fashion retail market in India.[9] Quitting such a successful enterprise should have been the last thing on Jain's mind. But as if he'd foreseen the bloodbath that was to follow in Indian e-commerce, Jain decided to jump ship and leave Jabong while the going was still good. In hindsight, one can only admire Jain's intuition for, as luck would have it, Jabong's fortunes started sinking soon after his resignation. A funding winter added to the woes of dozens of e-commerce companies, and many started shutting shop. In May 2014, Flipkart acquired Myntra, another big online fashion retail platform, for $280 million.[10] This mega acquisition was big news in the Indian e-commerce industry, and all eyes were fixed on what Flipkart's rival Jabong

---

8   https://www.inmobi.com/company/press/SoftBank-Corp-invests-
    200mn-in-InMobi-One-of-the-largest-investments-in-the/

9   https://qz.com/india/741485/the-rise-and-fall-of-jabong-is-the-future-
    for-many-other-indian-e-commerce-companies/

10 https://en.wikipedia.org/wiki/Flipkart

would do. In November 2014, *Business Standard* reported that Amazon was considering buying Jabong for $1.2 billion in order to 'counter Flipkart's move'.[11] However, the Amazon deal did not materialize. Meanwhile, Jabong, which had maintained a healthy competition with Myntra so far, found it increasingly difficult to keep up because of the Flipkart acquisition. Rocket Internet was also turning wary of investing more into the market. Now that Flipkart was pumping millions of dollars into Myntra to promote sales, Jabong could no longer rival its old competitor like before. With Jabong's declining performance and the Amazon deal falling through, its market value started to drop drastically. At one point, Flipkart proposed to pay $250 million to buy out Jabong, but like the last time, this acquisition did not happen either. In September 2015, Jabong's two other co-founders and Jain's former business partners, Praveen Sinha and Arun Chandra Mohan, quit Jabong after it reported heavy losses of ₹454 crore in the 2014 financial year filings.[12] Eventually, Flipkart did acquire Jabong in 2016—but for a paltry $70 million. In February 2020, Flipkart shut down Jabong to be able to focus better on Myntra.[13] Indeed, after tasting all that success in its initial days, for Jabong, the world, as it is said, didn't end with a bang but with a whimper. Jain could not have timed his exit any better.

11 https://www.indiainfoline.com/article/news-top-story/retail-newsletter-november-24-to-28-2014-114112801969_1.html

12 https://economictimes.indiatimes.com/industry/services/retail/jabong-confirms-exit-of-cofounder-arun-chandra-mohan/articleshow/48976231.cms?from=mdr

13 https://www.livemint.com/companies/news/flipkart-shuts-down-fashion-portal-jabong-to-focus-fully-on-myntra-11580961318073.html

As Jain was exiting Jabong by the end of 2013, senior executives at Xiaomi busied themselves with plans for a possible global expansion. Barra headed up the discussion on what steps lay ahead of Xiaomi's world conquest. India, as an important emerging market, became a top choice for Xiaomi. Given Lin Bin's recent friendship with Jain, their routine correspondences and, of course, Jain's rich knowledge of India's growing e-commerce business, Jain became a person of interest in matters relating to Xiaomi's business in India.

By then, Lin had known Jain for a year even though they had not met in person. That changed when the two met over coffee for the first time. Jain met with Xiaomi's leadership on their trip to India and was sold on the vision. He joined the company in May 2014. Jain later recalled how most of his friends and other industry experts had discouraged him from joining Xiaomi. They had good reason to do so. In 2014, only 6 per cent of India's market was online and Xiaomi's plans of pushing sales exclusively using online sales and word-of-mouth publicity seemed like a flawed strategy. Even Jain's own company, Jabong, spent big on marketing and sales promotions. In 2014, the *Economic Times* reported how Indian e-commerce companies were spending massively on TV ads. 'They may have been operating on shoestring budgets out of garages or home-offices till just a couple of years ago, but in recent months several Indian e-commerce firms including Flipkart, Jabong, and Quikr have emerged big spenders on TV commercials,' the report stated.[14] This was not always the case. In 2010-11, these companies spent

---

14 https://economictimes.indiatimes.com/industry/services/retail/
    online-retailers-like-flipkart-jabong-and-quikr-spending-massively-on-
    television-ads/articleshow/32809461.cms?from=mdr

no more than ₹10 lakh each on traditional advertisements, but by 2014, that budget had grown to somewhere between ₹25 crore and ₹75 crore. The rationale was pretty straightforward—in a country like India, whose population was predominantly offline, advertisements on traditional print and audio-visual mediums were the best strategies to foster online shopping habits. In light of this, Jain's bet on Xiaomi seemed like career suicide. 'In fact, some people told me, "You are making the biggest mistake of your life. Before it becomes public that you joined this company, leave it,"' Jain told a newspaper in a 2019 interview.[15] Xiaomi's zero-dollar approach to marketing was thoroughly untested outside China. Moreover, Chinese companies were a big no-no to work at for most Indian executives at the time.

No flash in the pan

Jain joined Xiaomi India as managing director in May 2014, just months before its official launch. This marked the second 'significant (international) hire' in Xiaomi's history since Barra's appointment in October 2013. On 11 June 2014, *Economic Times* ran a report that read, 'China's Xiaomi hires Jabong co-founder Manu Jain to head India operations'.[16] That very month the Xiaomi India Facebook page went live. Very quickly it got some 10,000 likes. This was a signal that Xiaomi could garner fans in India at very short notice and without traditional advertisements. Based on the response of Mi Fans on Xiaomi India's Facebook

15 https://www.livemint.com/mint-lounge/features/manu-kumar-jain-the-smartphone-man-11575603402395.html

16 https://economictimes.indiatimes.com/chinas-xiaomi-hires-jabong-co-founder-manu-jain-to-head-india-operations/articleshow/36367049.cms

page, the company decided to ship 10,000 handsets from China. The logic was simple—if each of the 10,000 fans bought a device, Manu and his team would have successfully sold out the entire inventory.

Until a few months earlier, Xiaomi hadn't quite decided on launching in India. But India's home-grown e-commerce firm Flipkart was looking to sew up exclusive deals with phone brands in a bid to ratchet up sales, and its founders Sachin Bansal and Binny Bansal had been to China to talk to Xiaomi. Mihir Dalal wrote in his 2019 book *Big Billion Startup: The Untold Flipkart Story*:[17]

> 'The Bansals had, in fact, been to China primarily to put the seal on a partnership with Xiaomi. Flipkart's sales team had been courting Xiaomi executives, urging them to sign an exclusive partnership. The hugely successful Moto G phone launch had changed the way brands looked at Flipkart; smartphone-makers that had earlier rejected its exclusivity request were now eager to pursue such an arrangement. But for Flipkart, securing a deal with Xiaomi was paramount, as its executives believed that these Chinese phones would enthral Indian shoppers.'

After several meetings between Lei and the Flipkart founders, the deal was sealed in July 2014.

Xiaomi picked the Mi3 device for its debut run, and the whole inventory sold out in exactly five seconds, creating a lot of hype and excitement among its Indian customers.

---

17 Mihir Dalal, *Big Billion Startup: The Untold Flipkart Story*. New Delhi: Macmillan, 2019.

Economic Times reported Flipkart officials saying that 'the traffic load at 2 p.m. on Tuesday afternoon when the sale began, was 4 times higher than the heaviest level ever experienced by Flipkart's infrastructure'.[18]

The Xiaomi flash sale in collaboration with Flipkart was unprecedented in the history of online sales in India. Previously, Motorola had done a similar sale, but no one had sold 10,000 phones in a matter of seconds as Xiaomi did. Flipkart's website crashed, but the company had just changed the dynamics of mobile phone retailing in the country. Flash sales became a popular mode of sales, and Flipkart, Amazon and Snapdeal competed for exclusives for years to come. For e-commerce companies, mobile phone sales became a way to quickly show top-line growth, and they chased after brands to bag exclusive rights to sell devices.

In the days preceding the big launch, the Xiaomi team in India had distributed Mi phones among a whole bunch of tech bloggers, YouTubers and journalists as a publicity exercise. Everybody had good things to say about the device. The Mi3, which was the only device being offered for the launch sale, was modestly priced at ₹13,999, keeping in mind the price-sensitive nature of Indian consumers. Other comparable devices cost upwards of ₹25,000 at the time. The phone's modest pricing, along with the glowing reviews from bloggers, organically created a lot of buzz around the time of launch. Top gadget-blogger Ranjit Kumar said the following about the device:

'If you take the price to performance ratio, this Xiaomi Mi3 just comes at the top. There's no other Android

---

18 https://economictimes.indiatimes.com/tech/hardware/xiaomis-mi3-sold-out-in-5-seconds-says-flipkart/articleshow/39250575.cms?from=mdr

device that can compete with this as of now if you take the overall price and performance into consideration. But again, Xiaomi is a new entrant in India and, as I told you, they have a limited amount [sic] of service centers and only time will tell how they can perform.'

Flipkart also drove traffic to the website to make the launch a success. Around 500,000 people registered for the flash sale, which had an inventory of just 10,000 phones! In other words, this launch had disaster written all over it. Flipkart scaled up its services, anticipating a hike in online traffic, but despite everything, the website crashed in the middle of the sale, leaving thousands of fans angry and dejected. The original sale took place on 22 July 2014. The following day, Jain told reporters, 'We underestimated the demand we would receive, and we are taking steps to ramp up the supply as soon as possible.'[19] Moreover, to placate aggrieved fans who had registered for the sale but could not purchase a phone, Jain promised to be back with another sale in a week's time on 29 July. By then, one thing was clear—Xiaomi's controversial yet extremely popular hunger marketing strategy and affordable pricing had worked in India.

This time, Flipkart did not take any chances and rebuilt its tech platform in a week to handle incoming traffic. Rashmi Bansal, the author of *Shine Bright*, a book featuring Jain as one of India's leading entrepreneurs, described this episode in graphic detail.

---

19 https://www.financialexpress.com/archive/sale-of-xiaomis-mi3-that-crashed-flipkart-resumes/1275053/

Speaking about the day on which Xiaomi hosted the second flash sale, Rashmi wrote,

> 'On D-day, Manu Jain was with Sachin Bansal [co-founder and the then CEO of Flipkart] at the Flipkart office, counting down the seconds. At exactly 2 pm, he pressed the "buy now" button. The message on the screen was "out of stock". *Oof! Site phir se crash ho gaya?* (Oh man, did the site crash again?) This was disappointing. But then the Flipkart team broke the good news. "Your entire stock—10,000 units—sold out in the first 2 seconds!"[20]

As demand grew following the two-second sell-out, Xiaomi chartered planes to transport inventory from China to India.

The company decided to ramp up production at the back end and bring fresh supplies to meet the demand of queued-up customers over another flash sale, which too met with a similar response. Commenting on the deluge of positive responses from Xiaomi's Indian fans, Jain said, 'We're pleasantly surprised by the numbers we saw today. There were an estimated 2.5 lakh customers on the site at the time of the sale.'[21] Manu's ambitions, along with Xiaomi's, grew. The plan now was to sell 10,000 phones a week. And in a few months, the company took aim at selling 100,000 phones a week.

Little did anyone know that Xiaomi's successful India debut was going to be awkwardly suspended in the coming months.

---

20 https://scroll.in/article/926490/entrepreneur-to-employee-manu-jains-reverse-journey-of-success-with-xiaomi-in-india

21 https://economictimes.indiatimes.com/tech/hardware/xiaomis-mi3-sold-out-in-5-seconds-says-flipkart/articleshow/39250575.cms?from=mdr

The Chinese company's woes began sooner than anticipated when it was served with a lawsuit in the winter of 2014. Swedish telecom giant Ericsson slapped a case against Xiaomi in December 2014 at the Delhi High Court, alleging that the Chinese start-up had committed patent infringement on eight counts, thus halting Xiaomi's India sales temporarily. Xiaomi's lack of patent portfolio continued to be a bone of contention over the years as it entered new markets and encountered bigger rivals. In this particular case, Ericsson alleged that Xiaomi was using MediaTek chipsets for which it owed a licensing fee. The Delhi High Court arbitrated the case and ordered Xiaomi to 'deposit ₹100 towards royalty for every device it imported to India from the date of the launch of the device in India to January 5, 2015. This amount was to be kept in a fixed deposit for three months during the proceeding of the case.'[22] Xiaomi was banned from selling devices in India. But it appealed against the injunction and said that the company also sold phones that ran on handsets with Qualcomm chipsets, which had already licensed technology from Ericsson. The court allowed Xiaomi to sell Qualcomm-based devices in a ruling on 16 December 2014. Following the setback caused by the lawsuit, Xiaomi quickly resumed operations in India, ready to roll out newer devices to its growing fanbase. Senior officials at Xiaomi resolved to bolster its patent portfolio, but overall the Ericsson lawsuit helped everyone realize that the company was resilient enough to take on future challenges. In 2019, Ericsson and Xiaomi signed a global patent licence agreement and laid the matter to rest.

---

22 https://www.khuranaandkhurana.com/2015/04/29/recent-patent-litigation-cases-2014-15-india/

The Ericsson lawsuit wasn't the only challenge Xiaomi faced in India. In October 2014, *Financial Express* broke a story that read, 'Desist from using Xiaomi'. Xiaomi devices, it was alleged, were transferring data back to their servers in China. This allegation, if found true, would be a huge security breach for the country and a big blow to Xiaomi's overseas business. It further added that 'F-secure, a leading security solution company, had recently carried out a test of Xiaomi Redmi 1s, the company's budget smartphone, and found that the phone was forwarding carrier name, phone number, IMEI [the device identifier] plus numbers from address book and text messages back to Beijing.'[23] In response, Hugo Barra clarified that 'the data that Xiaomi phone occasionally sent to Chinese servers was related to the company's cloud services. These services were opt in and could be turned off by users.'[24]

Despite reassurances, the backlash from the Indian army caused Xiaomi some reputation damage. More importantly, this incident reinstated the wariness about Chinese products in the hearts of its Indian users. Barely three months after the resounding success of its two-second flash sale, Xiaomi was back to square one, once again building a reputation for itself in the Indian market.

From sell in India, to make in India

The Xiaomi India office at this time operated out of a small workplace in Bengaluru with only six employees, including the

23 https://www.financialexpress.com/archive/desist-from-using-xiaomi-redmi-1s-indian-air-force-asks-its-personnel/1301632/

24 https://www.indiatoday.in/technology/news/story/our-phones-are-safe-iaf-notice-based-on-two-month-old-report-xiaomi-224320-2014-10-23

managing director, Jain. As a way to redeem Xiaomi's image and forge stronger engagement with fans and users, Jain took two crucial decisions. First, he started working proactively to associate Xiaomi with the Government of India's newly minted 'Make in India' campaign. Secondly, as a way to better connect with users, he started getting directly involved in the promotion of Mi fan communities across the country. Both would have a profound impact on Xiaomi's future in India.

The Government of India had launched the Make in India campaign in September 2014 as a way to attract more investments into the country, encouraging multinational companies to manufacture domestically, and in the process, create more jobs here. Nearly a million Indians reach the employable age of fifteen every month in India, and creating jobs was a priority for the government. This was a huge opportunity for Xiaomi India to rebuild its reputation, and Jain lost no time getting behind the initiative. Soon after, he started making frequent trips to India's capital city New Delhi to hold meetings with the ministers concerned, and by February 2015, talks of setting up Xiaomi's first manufacturing plant in India had already begun. This was a huge step that worked well for both sides. The Bharatiya Janata Party (BJP), which had freshly formed the government following a landslide victory in the 2014 national elections, was counting on the Make in India project to create jobs and bring in foreign investments. Getting a successful Chinese start-up to set up factories in India would no doubt be considered a great achievement, and so the BJP government welcomed this proposal with great enthusiasm. Xiaomi, too, realized how this deal would benefit tremendously from the support it would receive from the government—it would not only help them regain the goodwill of the people, but also make business in India a lot more profitable.

Xiaomi was the first smartphone brand to start assembling smartphones in India under the Make in India programme. But it was not the only brand that joined the initiative. In June 2015, the *Indian Express* reported that the initiative was less about patriotism and more about 'sound economics'. Evidently, many smartphone makers, both domestic and foreign, had been responding to Prime Minister Narendra Modi's call to set up manufacturing plants in India. Apart from Xiaomi, Indian brands such as Micromax and Lava, Chinese brand Oppo and even the South Korean electronics giant Samsung had begun setting up manufacturing facilities in India. Assembling the product in India made more economic sense than importing a finished product into India. This was because 'while a smartphone attracts a duty of around 12.5 per cent, its components can be imported at just 1 per cent. Mobile manufacturing companies are trying to take advantage of this massive skew in the duty structure—it makes sense for them to assemble in India,' the report explained.[25] The more components were imported and assembled in India, the better the profit margins would become. The policy measure of giving companies 'production linked incentives' has indeed created a better electronics manufacturing ecosystem in the country. Between 2015 - 2020, more than 200 mobile manufacturing units have been set up in India. Together, they've produced 330 million devices, worth over $30 billion, the government has said.

---

25 https://indianexpress.com/article/explained/its-economics-the-reason-smartphone-makers-are-taking-the-make-in-india-call/

In late April 2015, Lei Jun visited India during the launch of the Mi 4i smartphone. It was the first time Xiaomi announced a phone in India first. Back then, the Xiaomi India office comprised a small team. Lei spent a lot of time with employees strategizing what the next move was going to be. But he was also keen to experience the Indian market so as to have a better understanding of what his consumers wanted. He set off to explore the market scene, visiting bazaars and malls alike, trying to gauge what the Indian shopper was looking for. Before leaving, Lei had one unconventional suggestion for the senior executives at the India office—he asked them to start hiring Mi Fans as Xiaomi employees. Lei had always aspired to head a 'cool' company. To that end, he wished for his users to be more than just consumers. A fan was truly passionate about a company's products and a real brand loyalist. To Lei, it made a lot of sense to channel that energy into the actual work of Xiaomi's day-to-day operations. He felt if fans worked at their favourite company, they would be more motivated to deliver results than a regular employee ever would. Xiaomi's fourth employee in India was Rohit Ghalsasi, who was originally a Mi Fan and had a community of Xiaomi fans even before the phones were officially launched in India. Ghalsasi, who took the job in his early twenties, continues to work at the company even after six years at Xiaomi.

A great validation for Xiaomi's strategy in India came as early as 2015 in the form of personal investment from Ratan Tata, one of India's top industrialists. Lei Jun announced the investment on his visit to India in 2015 and said, 'Mr. Tata is one of the most well-respected business leaders in the world. An investment by him is an affirmation of the strategy we have undertaken in India so far.'[26]

In August 2015, Xiaomi announced that it was opening its first manufacturing unit in Sri City in Andhra Pradesh. Sri City was a newly developed industrial township. Lying at the border of Andhra Pradesh and only 65km from Chennai, this sprawling special economic zone (SEZ) of 1,089 hectares that had started being developed only in 2007 was already host to 165 companies from twenty-seven countries, including Kellogg's, Colgate-Palmolive, Foxconn and PepsiCo. The Redmi 2, which was part of the super affordable range of smartphones priced at ₹6,999, was going to be the first Xiaomi phone to be assembled here. As the chief guest at the launch in Visakhapatnam, Andhra Pradesh Chief Minister Chandrababu Naidu said,

'We have great faith in young leaders and young companies like Xiaomi. These new generation companies and entrepreneurs will be key to the success of Andhra Pradesh and India. We are happy to partner with Xiaomi as they set up their first manufacturing unit in India as part of the Make in India programme. We believe this partnership will provide new opportunities to the youth of the state and develop an electronics-manufacturing ecosystem of global standards in Andhra Pradesh.'[27]

---

26 https://www.reuters.com/article/us-indian-company-tata-sons/indias-ratan-tata-buys-stake-in-chinese-phone-maker-xiaomi-idUSKBN0NH04S20150426

27 https://www.digit.in/press-release/mobile-phones/xiaomi-will-make-in-india-out-of-andhra-plant-26789.html

Also present was Barra, who said,

'We kicked off our conversations with Chief Minister Chandrababu Naidu in China. Here we are now. What we thought would've taken us two years, we have done it in six months. Manufacturing in India for Xiaomi is a "Just in Time" opportunity. Over a period of time, every single phone Xiaomi sells in India will be made in India. We are proud to be the first movers into India. What's happening in India is incredible. Internet Revolution ... We are proud to be at the forefront of the "Make in India" program.'[28]

In late 2019, Xiaomi claimed that nearly 99 per cent of the phones it sold in India were 'made' in India. Xiaomi had partnered with Taiwanese manufacturing giant Foxconn and Flex. While this is commendable, a more accurate version is that 65 per cent of the components were sourced from India, and the plants in India assembled the devices. About 85 per cent of Mi TVs and all the powerbanks by Xiaomi are made in India. This has generated more than 30,000 jobs and was clearly seen as a win for the Make in India programme.

Xiaomi had always been a big believer in competitive pricing. With the opening of the manufacturing facility at Sri City, prices of Mi phones were expected to drop even lower as local production was going to be cheap and stocks could be replenished faster. Better prices meant more sales. As sales grew exponentially, India

28 Ibid.

was well on its way to becoming Xiaomi's second-largest market after China.

The niche that Xiaomi India had carved for itself through all of 2015 soon started to grow. The year 2016 saw Xiaomi emerge as a big player in the Indian smartphone business. Barely two years since it began its operations in India, Xiaomi touched $1 billion in revenue. Jain took this opportunity to go on Facebook to share the news with Mi Fans. He wrote, 'Based on what we know, we are the first company to cross $1 billion in such a short period.'

This was not all. The year 2016 saw Xiaomi touch a few other milestones. Television channel NDTV said Xiaomi had sold over 2 million smartphones in the country, becoming one of the top three smartphone brands in India and accomplishing a 150 per cent year-on-year growth since 2015. Additionally, the popular Redmi Note 3 had sold 2.3 million devices in just six months, 'making the Xiaomi smartphone the most shipped device being sold online'. There was more. Jain also announced that 'the Xiaomi Redmi 3S [and Xiaomi Redmi 3S Prime], and Redmi Note 3 were the top selling devices during Flipkart's Big Billion Days, and Amazon's Great Indian Sale, respectively.' It was true. Xiaomi was no longer selling exclusively through Flipkart but also used the Amazon and Snapdeal platforms to push online sales in India. Its own platform, mi.com, was also seeing a lot of traffic. Overall, Xiaomi seemed to have covered its ground pretty well in the online sales department and with little money spent on traditional advertising, to boot. Even while Xiaomi was riding high, Jain and his team built relationships in New Delhi. In 2017, during another visit to India, Lei Jun met with Prime Minister Narendra Modi and presented a plaque that contained the components of the Xiaomi Redmi Note 3, a phone Xiaomi made in India. A few years later in 2020, when tensions between India and China would escalate, Jain's efforts to build bridges in New Delhi would pay off.

Online is great, but why miss offline sales?

By now it was clear that Xiaomi was a champion at its online sales strategy. However, despite experiencing a great boost in e-commerce sales, Xiaomi was still unreachable to most Indians. Nearly two-thirds of the country's population remained offline. Towards late 2015 and through 2016, India's overall e-commerce growth had also started showing signs of slowing down. As a way to reach out to the largely offline population, in early 2017, Xiaomi India decided to enter the offline market. This meant renting retail spaces in smaller towns and tier-two cities so that consumers who did not have sufficient online access could buy Mi products from retail outlets. Accordingly, Jain and his team contacted the manager at a Bengaluru shopping mall in order to book a space in the establishment. Jain had expected this to be a quick meeting, but the mall manager had other ideas! At the Insights Podcast hosted by Accel in September 2019, Jain regaled listeners with stories of how the mall manager refused to give them a shop of their liking (a big showroom, preferably on the ground floor of the mall) since he staunchly believed that Xiaomi's tremendous online popularity could not be replicated in an offline scenario. Resigning himself to the manager's advice, a reluctant Jain decided to take the deal. Thus, despite having grand plans, a 600-square-foot basement store in Bengaluru's Phoenix Market City Mall eventually became India's first Xiaomi outlet, or Mi Home, as they came to be called. The mall manager had earlier told Jain he would be surprised if a hundred people turned up at the shop on the day of the launch. Jain was not going to let a basement shop spoil Xiaomi's big launch and decided to do something unconventional. To draw customers, the shop's opening was planned to coincide with the launch of a new phone model, the Redmi 4. In fact, the device was made available at the store a day before it went live for online sales. On D-day, 20 May 2017, nearly 10,000 people turned up at the shop for the launch, many travelling long distances from outside Bengaluru, including one man from Gujarat who came with a bag full of cash to buy twenty phones! That day Xiaomi sold phones worth nearly $1 million from the 600-square-foot shop, proving that Xiaomi could perform just as well through offline sales as it had done via online platforms. Over time, some 6,000 stores opened up across the country, most of them raking in profits within the first five to six months. The move to go offline was particularly useful in reaching out to consumers in tier-two cities who were migrating to smartphones around this time.

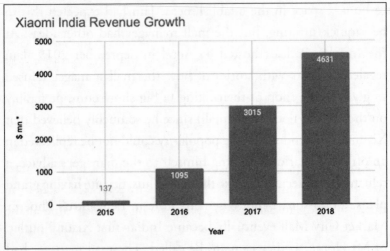

Source: Company filings, Ministry of Corporate Affairs.

Once the offline business took off, Xiaomi India started looking for ways to generate more revenue through its retail outlets. It struck deals with local retailers to increase its presence in smaller towns and cities. 'Here, again, Xiaomi went directly to the retailer, cutting out the distributors in between. It now sells offline in over 40 cities and has more than 4,000 preferred partners who sell Xiaomi phones. It also launched in large format retailers that year with Sangeeta, Poorvika, Croma and Reliance Digital,' *FactorDaily* reported.[29] By the end of 2017, '25% of the company's sales were from offline channels across over a dozen Indian cities'. Additionally, India's metro cities now had Xiaomi showrooms, the Mi Home that exclusively sold Xiaomi devices, including power banks and air purifiers, with plans to set up smaller Mi homes in more cities in the coming years. By the end of 2019, nearly half of Xiaomi India's revenues were expected to come from offline channels. Xiaomi now operates more than 2,500 Mi Stores, 75 Mi Homes and 20 Mi Studios. It has over 7,000 Mi Preferred Partner stores across the country.

By this time, the control from Beijing headquarters had loosened considerably, and the India team was at liberty to take decisions concerning everyday administration. This was especially caused by the boost in sales following the introduction of the Redmi series, with a price range starting from ₹5,499 and going up to ₹28,999, which instantly hit a sweet spot among customers from different income brackets in terms of both strategy and product pricing. Even so, senior officials from China continued to visit the Bengaluru office at regular intervals. In fact, until his resignation in early 2017, Barra spent so much time at the

---

29 Ibid.

Bengaluru office that he jokingly called it his second home. With Barra's resignation, Jain was promoted as the vice president of Xiaomi Global though he continued to focus on India. With time, his responsibilities were further expanded to accommodate the rest of the subcontinent. Accordingly, in January 2018, Jain became the managing director of the Indian subcontinent, which includes India, Bangladesh, Sri Lanka, Nepal and Bhutan—a portfolio that's growing over time.

Jain turned thirty-seven in 2018. In just four years at Xiaomi he had raised himself from managing the company's business in India to a much larger role overseeing the company's South Asia business. His colleagues, including former employees at Xiaomi India, agree that Jain is a highly driven and ambitious person who is never too tired to learn something new. 'He has amazing networking skills and always manages to leverage the right connections'. Aside from the good things his fellow employees say about him, the revenue numbers for 2018 also showed that Xiaomi India was in good shape. The company booked revenues of ₹35,427 crore (~$5 bn) in revenue in 2019, a 54 per cent growth from the previous year. Xiaomi had seen phenomenal growth and was showing no signs of stopping. It had already emerged as the leading smartphone in India, beating Samsung in the final quarter of 2017. TechCrunch wrote, 'Data from both analyst houses [Canalys and Counterpoint] gave Xiaomi a narrow lead over Samsung in the final quarter of 2017, with 27 percent and 25 percent, respectively, according to Canalys—and 25 percent versus 23 percent, according to Counterpoint.'[30]

---

30 https://techcrunch.com/2018/01/25/xiaomi-samsung-india/

Riding that wave of success, in 2018, Jain and his team in India did something unprecedented—they opened over 500 retail stores across rural areas of the country in a single day, setting the Guinness Book of World Records for the maximum number of stores opened in twenty-four hours! Present for the award ceremony, a beaming Jain told reporters that Xiaomi had plans of opening another 5,000 stores by the end of 2019, which would potentially create 15,000 jobs in rural areas. Of course, no one foresaw that a pandemic would throw a spanner in the works soon.

On Xiaomi's website, among the many Chinese faces you will spot the unmistakable Indian face of Manu Jain. That to an average browser may not mean much, but for those who know of Xiaomi's success in India, it is clear that the spot is hard earned. From fighting prejudices against Chinese products to establishing themselves as India's most-loved smartphone brand to creating jobs, Xiaomi's India story in these years has been a truly amazing one. The man from a humble trading family in Meerut was now at the forefront of a smartphone revolution and a top executive at a trailblazing company.

Chapter 5
Fans with Benefits

Y EARS BEFORE LEI JUN founded Xiaomi, he had one simple dream—he wanted to build a 'cool' company. Xiaomi's stated mission is to 'be friends with our users. Be the coolest company in the hearts of our users.' Redeeming the image of China as the country of cheap knock-offs and cheap labour was, of course, part of the larger plan. But, fundamentally, Lei envisioned a company that was founded upon friendship. The photo of Xiaomi's co-founders—Lei Jun, Lin Bin, Li Wanqiang, among others—huddled over a pot of steaming millet porridge is symbolic of this friendship. In spite of the sepia tint and grainy texture, the photo seen on social media reveals an indisputable fact—these men were friends first, business partners later. The importance of friendship did not lose relevance when it came to Xiaomi's users, either. Lei, and indeed the rest who dreamt along with him, had always insisted on becoming friends with their consumers. For instance, at times after opening a new store,

Xiaomi employees would celebrate with fans in the locality over millet porridge. This was no marketing gimmick. From day one until now, Xiaomi has prioritized its users, tried to understand them, and most importantly, *indulge* them. Xiaomi's success is owed to several factors. From competitive pricing to low profit margins, Xiaomi has checked off all the boxes that make for a successful business. But ultimately, if there has been one thing that has truly set this company apart, it is a unique user model.

Xiaomi has been called a copycat many times, especially that it tries to copy Apple. But that is largely an uninformed view. Sure, it has borrowed some aesthetic aspects from Apple Inc. An unwritten but often followed rule at Xiaomi is that the products it makes should aesthetically pair well when kept next to an Apple product. But in reality, it operates with a radically different philosophy from the makers of the iPhone. Apple's design process is largely top-down, whereas Xiaomi's design process is radically bottom-up. The Chinese company, which wants to bring 'innovation to everyone', has its ear close to the ground. It listens to its users intensely, and that gives it a unique advantage over competitors. As you look back at Xiaomi's ten years, it becomes clearer that the secret sauce, or the binding force in all of Xiaomi's endeavours, is its users.

The idea of becoming friends with the users did not come out of the blue. We all know of companies that boast of being a 'big, happy family'. Yet, Xiaomi officials have never compared their employees or their users with families. The logic behind this is perhaps simpler than it appears—you are born *into* a family, but you *choose* your friends. By striving to become friends with their employees and customers, Xiaomi sent out a deep message—it was going to build a business model where people willingly *chose* to be associated with their brand and not the other way around. This approach would help Xiaomi win the market that was already crowded. When Xiaomi emerged in 2010, China's mobile phone industry was already booming, with total smartphone sales estimated to be around 30 million units.[1] Nokia still held on to half the market with a 50.3 per cent share, HTC was at 9.8 per cent, Samsung at 9.2 per cent, Motorola at 8.4 per cent, Apple at 6.1 per cent, while the remaining 16.2 per cent belonged to a cluster comprising Blackberry, LG and Lenovo. That year China's biggest private company Huawei, which was primarily a telecom equipment manufacturer, stepped up its focus on smartphones as well. Although Huawei started a handset division in 2003, its first Android smartphone was showcased at the Mobile World Congress in 2009.[2]

Nokia and Motorola, as we know, were almost on their way out after struggling for years to transition from the feature phone era to the smartphone era while Apple, which launched in China more than a year after its original launch in the Western market, was not only expensive but also a very new phenomenon for the middle-class Chinese consumers. Of all these brands, South Korean giant Samsung, standing with a modest 9.2 per cent of the market share in 2010, was going to grow exponentially over the next few years, becoming a huge entity not just in China but also across the world. Apple would also eventually become a big success in China as the country's population became wealthier.

---

1 https://www.nanjingmarketinggroup.com/blog/china-smartphones/2010-2011-china-smartphone-market-overview

2 https://www.phonearena.com/news/Huawei-showcases-its-first-Android-powered-smartphone_id4129

Samsung's business model was deeply entrenched in the idea of building products that exceeded the consumers' imagination. In 2012, the company's homepage said, 'Samsung Electronics is like an inventor for trends that change our lives. Its features and designs transform my days with exciting creative experiences that I never before imagined. I find new ways to live with Samsung Electronics.' The messaging clearly positioned Samsung as a company that saw ahead of the curve and created products that fit into that vision of the future. When Xiaomi came along, it decided to turn this model on its head. In his book *The Xiaomi Way*, Li Wanqiang, one of Xiaomi's co-founders, talks about the thought process that went into developing Xiaomi's basic outlook. 'It's not a matter of implanting our thought into the consumers' consciousness,' Li wrote in the book, which was first published in Chinese and later translated to English, 'It is a matter of infiltrating consumers' consciousness to obtain their thought.'[3] Implanting a new idea or thought into the users' minds was what Samsung sought to achieve when it introduced a new and innovative product in the market. Instead, Xiaomi chose to draw inspiration *from* the minds of its consumers and develop a product that met their needs. It put the users' needs right at the centre of product development and tried to incorporate their ideas into its products.

Xiaomi's fan based approach to marketing is an antidote to the wariness that customers have developed to traditional advertising. As marketing guru Philip Kotler points out this changing customer behaviour in his book Marketing 4.0 — Moving from Traditional to Digital, 'They're (customers)

---

3   Li Wanqiang, *The Xiaomi Way*, op. citation.

becoming increasingly wary of marketing communications from brands and are relying instead on the F factor: friends, families, fans and followers. Finally, the customer buying process is becoming more social than it has been previously. Customers are paying more attention to their social circle in making decisions. They seek advice and reviews both online and offline.'[4]

Unlike before, listening closely to users had become critical to business. In hindsight, an episode from Nokia's journey is instructive in this regard. When Nokia, under former Microsoft executive Stephen Elop, decided to kill its proprietary operating system Symbian and make Microsoft its primary smartphone operating system in 2010, it read its users completely wrong. Elop later told journalists that the decision was driven by concerns of market domination by one player, potential to negotiate with carriers, Microsoft's ability to create an alternative to iOS and Android and several other business considerations.[5] This not only alienated diehard Nokia fans who liked Symbian for all its flaws but also completely ignored the fact that users had gone hoarse asking Nokia to build Android phones. The move, ignoring users, cost Nokia dearly as the future of smartphones dictated by the users clearly became a two-horse race between Android and iOS. Clinton Jeff, one of the early gadget reviewers in India who went on to work for Xiaomi, said:

'True Nokia fans were like, "What are you doing!" You have this nice operating system and you're not choosing that.

---

4   Philip Kotler, Hermawan Kartajaya, Iwan Setiawan. *Marketing 4.0: Moving from Traditional to Digital*. New Jersey: John Wiley, 2017.

5   https://www.theguardian.com/technology/2013/jul/12/elop-explains-nokia-android

You're going with Microsoft operating system because you assume they will put money behind building a competitor to Android. He [Elop] just thought that this makes sense from a business perspective. But from a fan perspective, it was a complete no. At the same time, Samsung was coming up with Android phones and it was the closest you had to an iPhone experience, which the fans really wanted.'

Nokia eventually sold its handset division to Microsoft in a fire sale, and in January 2019, Microsoft officially stopped developing the Windows phone platform.[6]

The effect of siding squarely with the users, or rather democratically designing their product, was revolutionary. Not only did it help Xiaomi avoid big mistakes, but fans also made it easy for Xiaomi to globalize better. For instance, in China the company had a beauty filter on its camera app. But in India, because fans were strongly opposed to the idea, the company did not bring in that feature. Similarly, Indian fans clamoured for a radio frequency chip in the phone so that it could double as a remote control for the TV and other devices such as air conditioners, and this chip is now a regular feature of Xiaomi phones. Again, if you contrast this with Nokia, you'll see how revolutionary this seemingly simple philosophy of really listening to the users is. Nokia made a conscious choice to stick with a stylus even though the technology to support finger-based touch had been in existence for decades before the iPhone made it mainstream. The Finnish company's thinking, as one gadget reviewer posits, was that people in cold countries like Finland would have to take off their gloves

---

6   https://gadgets.ndtv.com/mobiles/news/nokia-ceo-explains-why-they-chose-windows-phone-over-android-394274

to operate the phone if not for a stylus. What this meant was that it had to choose resistive touchscreens. Resistive touchscreens, as opposed to capacitive touchscreens used in the iPhone, were not as sensitive and didn't support multi-touch gestures. But the truth is, the next generation of smartphone buyers were from countries such as India and China, where the weather is far warmer through most of the year. Even in the US, after the launch of the iPhone in 2007, capacitive touchscreens were undoubtedly proven to be the user-friendly choice. Had Nokia put fans at the core of its product development strategy, an overwhelming number of users would have told them that they wanted a touchscreen like the iPhone and not a stylus they'd lose often and needed two hands to work.

Xiaomi's business philosophy not only turned users into friends but also produced a community of loyal fans in a very short time.

'Good companies make profits, great companies also win over people's hearts. We pride ourselves even more in being a technology company with a rare "fan culture". We have a large global community of "Mi Fans", passionate users who are intensely loyal to our brand, highly engaged on our platform and actively contribute feedback and feature ideas to our product development.'

Lei wrote in his letter to shareholders a couple of months before Xiaomi's public listing.[7] This wasn't by any means a stretch of the imagination.

---

7   http://blog.mi.com/en/2018/05/03/open-letter-from-our-chairman/

'Xiaomi has built a vibrant user community, which is not common for products in this category. This reduces their marketing costs and also helps to keep interest in its products alive when they have no new launches,' says Jessie Paul, the author of *No Money Marketing* and a marketing specialist. Xiaomi has indeed managed to cultivate a global fan base. How did it achieve all this?

How Xiaomi roped in fan power

Xiaomi, as we know, did not start its journey as a smartphone manufacturer. Rather, it entered the business with its own operating system, the MIUI, which, when installed in existing phones, improved their efficiency considerably. MIUI had three central features—it was fast, it was smooth and, most importantly, it was open access. Lei Jun, who had until then worked at Kingsoft for a good part of his professional career, was used to spending months developing a product. With smartphones and operating systems, though, he realized that the turnaround time for product updates had to be a lot quicker. Recalling those days, Li Wanqiang wrote, 'R&D on the user experience was no longer a matter of monthly or quarterly meetings but rather a matter of daily communications with users.'[8] MIUI's bulletin boards allowed users to post reviews, comments and suggestions to regular software updates, which were then quickly incorporated into the operating system and made available in the next week's roll-out. Xiaomi kept in touch with its users on a bulletin board system (BBS) where user demands would

---

8   Li Wanqiang, The Xiaomi Way, op. cit.

bubble up to the top. Following this, small two- to three-member teams would work round the clock through the week to build features that had received the highest number of votes from users. Every Friday, known as Orange Friday, Xiaomi would ship a new version of MIUI. The urgency around product delivery in effect helped Xiaomi create a deeper bond with its users. Imagine being in 'daily communication' with your consumers; given the frequency of communication, Xiaomi's relationship with its users became intimate, organic and dialogue-based. The MIUI was fundamentally a great product, but the incorporation of user feedback made it even better. Indeed, within a year of launch, its subscribers shot up from 100 to 500,000. Xiaomi had successfully made them feel like they were an integral part of the development process. This was a very different approach from what Samsung and others had been pursuing. Instead of surprising its users with new products like everyone else, Xiaomi showed that it was, in fact, paying close attention to users' needs and building its products accordingly.

This proved to be a foolproof way to secure the loyalty of fans. By allowing them to participate in the process, Xiaomi created a sense of credibility and trustworthiness among users, who returned the favour with unwavering loyalty. The fans felt vested in seeing Xiaomi succeed.

In industry parlance, this phenomenon is known as participatory consumption, where users are not merely passive consumers but instead take on the role of direct participants. Outside the realm of smartphones and technology, the company that started thinking seriously about participatory consumption was the Swedish furniture company Ikea. Founded in 1943, Ikea's strength lies in its philosophy of integrating the consumer's labour directly into the furniture-building process. Ikea products do not come pre-assembled; they arrive in flat packs instead. This not only allows the company to save on packaging costs, but the flat packs also make it easier to transport the products. Over time, Ikea has built a reputation as a consumer-friendly company that sells ready-to-assemble pieces, allowing families and friends to come together, turning the mundane chore of assembling furniture into a fun do-it-yourself activity. In fact, Ikea is a great example of a participatory consumption model that has not only helped the company save on additional labour costs, but by letting consumers take part in the final assembly, they have, in effect, enabled consumers to *own* their products at a deep and emotional level—would-be parents setting up a crib for their child, or the first-time office goer furnishing her living room with friends. This unique psychological phenomenon has also received the attention of research scholars. In 2011, Michael L. Norton of Harvard Business School, Daniel Motion of Yale University and Dan Ariely of Duke University conducted a study where they identified this phenomenon as the 'Ikea Effect' in which buyers place 'a disproportionately high value on products they helped create'.[9] The Ikea Effect has been pervasive; in a FreemanXP article cheekily titled, 'Are your ideas really that good? Beware of the Ikea Effect', the author discusses how the 'effect' induces consumers to 'fall in love with their Ikea creations. Even when there are parts missing and the items are incorrectly built, customers in the Ikea study still loved the fruits of their labors.'[10] Almost like how you end up liking the dish you cooked, even if it's a little burnt. We

---

9   https://en.wikipedia.org/wiki/IKEA_effect
10   Ibid.

have all seen home videos of first-time dads building their child's playroom and young couples spending their weekends poring over the contents of the Ikea user's manual. Consumers have even engineered novel ways to tweak the instructions and design their own style of furniture. Popularly known as 'Ikea hacks', these are examples of participatory consumption where consumers have put up videos of their handiwork on YouTube, Pinterest and Instagram, bragging to their friends and followers about their newest Ikea invention.[11]

This is the logic that Xiaomi built into its own business model—it emphasized the significance of 'play' to optimize user engagement. As a smartphone and internet company, Xiaomi was quick to exploit the ubiquity of the device to its own advantage. In today's world, where an average person spends a large part of the day glued to their phone, Xiaomi introduced the idea of 'play' into its user-engagement model so that users would spend even longer hours on their Mi phones. A designer by training, co-founder Li Wanqiang, who was in charge of Xiaomi's branding and creative design, has always been attentive to the little features that distinguished Xiaomi from every other brand—'Users of other brands "use" their phones. The users of Mi "play with" their phones,' he said. However, making the interface playful and addictive was hardly fun and games and involved a lot of heavy lifting. Wanqiang's team ultimately came up with what he calls the 'three-on-three principles of engagement'—usefulness, emotional appeal and interactivity. It was these last two features—emotional appeal and interactivity—that made Xiaomi products stand out from the rest of the devices available in the

---

11   https://in.pinterest.com/beachbrights/ikea-hacks/

market. Xiaomi users were not simply using their products; rather, they were emotionally attached to their devices, which led them to spontaneously discuss its merits with their friends and family. This, in turn, helps create word-of-mouth endorsements, the most powerful validation a productmaker or marketer can hope for. This is also one of the ways in which Xiaomi turned word-of-mouth promotions into a great marketing strategy, but more on that later.

Participatory consumption: from Ikea to TikTok

If Ikea was one of the first non-tech companies to have successfully adopted the participatory consumption model, some others in the tech world too were deploying this method with varying degrees of success. The success of crowdfunding platforms is a great indicator of how the age of participatory consumption is truly upon us. Kickstarter is one of the most successful crowdfunding platforms today that recognizes and funds artisanal projects. With a mission to 'Help bring creative projects to life', Kickstarter requires project creators to develop a high degree of engagement with potential backers. Unlike in the past when companies exclusively marketed the finished goods, now marketing starts even before the goods have been manufactured. Today, it is more about engaging with the audience right from the idea stage. Building in public has proven to be hugely successful in many cases. The makers of the fidget cube, for instance, set out to raise $15,000 and ended up with over 150,000 backers who collectively made contributions exceeding $6 million! The Pebble watch is another great example that managed to raise more than $20 million on Kickstarter. This is a unique take on a classic patron-subscription model—one that comes with a democratic design, which is to say that projects are cancelled if they do not find enough backers to vote with their wallets by a set deadline. The fact that as of April 2020, over 181,141 projects have raised more than $4.9 billion on Kickstarter alone goes to show that a successful user-engagement model not only helps push sales but can also generate funding to kick-start exciting projects.[12]

Lego, the famous Danish toy company, too tried its hand at participatory consumption by way of democratizing its designs. In 2008, Lego collaborated with the Japanese company Cuusoo to offer a platform for consumers to create and vote for the most popular designs.[13] The most up-voted designs were then manufactured and sent out to the market as formal products. As an additional perk, the creator of the winning design was entitled to 1 per cent of the product revenue in royalties and copies of the final Lego set. Lego's crowdsourced design innovations became such a huge hit that in 2014 Lego bought out Cuusoo and renamed it Lego Ideas. Since then, Lego Ideas has become an interactive platform for Lego enthusiasts who are given daily activities and challenges that push them to come up with cool designs that fit the theme.

Ikea, Kickstarter and Lego aside, today a discussion on participatory consumption models would be incomplete without a mention of TikTok. A video-sharing social media platform, TikTok was founded in China in 2012. It became available

---

12　https://www.kickstarter.com/help/stats (last accessed on 26 April 2020)

13　https://digital.hbs.edu/platform-digit/submission/lego-ideas-crowdsourcing-the-next-big-hit/

to markets outside China in 2017 and later acquired a short video app called Musically to go bigger globally. In 2018, it was declared the most downloaded app in the US. By 2019, it had hit 1 billion downloads making it the seventh most downloaded app across the globe in the entire decade (2010–19). But how did the Chinese company become so popular? TikTok allows users to upload short lip-sync videos of three to fifteen seconds and longer looping videos of three to sixty seconds. Like most social media apps now, TikTok uses algorithms to determine users' preferences and personalizes content accordingly. But what has truly set TikTok apart is the array of features that lets users record their reactions to other videos, perform 'duets', share their creations with friends or make their videos available for public viewing. Perceived as a light-hearted, 'fun' app that allows users to recreate original music videos, TikTok has also enabled users and creators to even post sensitive content that would otherwise be censored on other video-sharing platforms. TikTok's user-centric model has been a smashing hit, with consumers spending an average of fifty-two minutes on the app every day. In an academic article in 2019, researcher Jiang Xiao Yu explained how the 'user-centric' approach of TikTok became such a massive success. Jiang wrote, 'TikTok enhance [sic] the deep interaction with the user, reconstructs the user connection, combine [sic] different scenarios to meet the user's information interaction and expression needs, provide customized services, achieve resource aggregation and value creation.' Not surprisingly, the Xiaomi model too has been founded upon these basic principles.

Xiaomi shows how a product can be turned into an activity and a company into a successful consumer-facing organization. From its early days as an operating system to becoming one of the most popular smartphone companies, Xiaomi has put its users first every step of the way. From getting user feedback on weekly software updates to hosting opinion polls for new features, and even employing Mi Fans as its employees, Xiaomi has become an internet company for the user, by the user and of the user.

Since most of Xiaomi's co-founders and other senior officials had earlier held positions in leading phone companies, including Motorola and Samsung, they were keenly aware of the problems plaguing the emerging smartphone industry. The industry, they realized, certainly had room for improvement. However, despite having several pain points in their operations, leading smartphone companies were neither paying heed to user complaints nor incorporating user suggestions into improving their devices at the rate at which customers were asking for improvements. A relative latecomer to the scene, Xiaomi used this opportunity to connect with users and offer them exactly what they had been demanding all along. The user-engagement model was designed keeping in mind the fundamental fact that 'users' as such did not comprise a homogenous unit. In 2019, researchers Mingwei Li, Suling Jia and Wenyu (Derek) Du argued in their paper that the fans were a rich source of Xiaomi's extended innovation capabilities:[14] Xiaomi divided users into four basic categories based on their individual skills and levels of expertise. These categories were slotted in descending order of technical skills with about 1,000 high-skilled developers, 100,000 medium- to high-skilled product testers and 350 medium-skilled product supporters. The fourth category, consisting of regular users, required a very low skill set (for posting

---

14 https://www.researchgate.net/publication/328090129_Fans_as_a_
    source_of_extended_innovation_capabilities_A_case_study_of_Xiaomi_
    Technology

new ideas and promoting new products) but drew in people from the first three categories as well. In marketing terms, the fourth category would be the top of the funnel. As is self-explanatory, the user-developers were invited to co-develop the system with Xiaomi engineers; product testers were in charge of beta testing and had to submit regular test reports; and product supporters were expected to spend an hour every day fielding questions from regular users about the best ways to use the system.

Why spend big money on advertising?

While the first three categories of users volunteered to improve MIUI, the Xiaomi operating system, and later entire devices, it was the fourth group that really took the gospel to the ends of the earth. From the very start, Xiaomi officials were clear about two things—one, they were not going to spend big money on advertisements and two, they were going to let their products speak for themselves. 'Don't create ads; create good content', or 'don't run ads; just use WeMedia', are some of the mantras that underpin Xiaomi's marketing philosophy. When Xiaomi first introduced its 'no ad' philosophy, it naturally created a stir in the industry. At a time when both Apple and Samsung, the two smartphone giants, were splurging on marketing, Xiaomi vowed to spend $0 on advertising. Indeed, the 'zero dollar' story itself got the whole industry talking about this new Chinese brand that was heading towards doom. But inside Xiaomi, executives knew that their fans would gladly spread the word for them. Li Wanqiang believed that the days of luring consumers via ad scripting were long over, and newer strategies had to be implemented to generate user interest. Accordingly, Xiaomi decided to create outreach through channels such as Weibo, the Chinese microblogging app. Instead of pushing paid ads to unsuspecting viewers, Xiaomi produced content that would naturally appeal to the public, create an organic form of engagement and go viral. It helped that Xiaomi's rise coincided with the rise of social media in China.

For one, unboxing videos became really popular. Taking the cue from tech bloggers and influencers, Xiaomi started posting unboxing videos of its devices to familiarize the audience with the basic features of the phone. It also started spending a lot of time, energy and money on producing well-designed and good quality products. For instance, while other companies spent just a few dollars on the packaging box, Xiaomi decided to use boxes that cost $10 apiece. A difference in price naturally brought a difference in quality. A Xiaomi box was so sturdy that it could support the weight of adult humans. To show this, Xiaomi once put up a light-hearted video of two brothers, both very portly, balancing themselves on top of a Xiaomi box. The video went viral thanks to Mi Fans. The sight of two large people balancing themselves atop a small box was bound to evoke laughter. By posting this video on their Weibo page, Xiaomi transformed a passive audience into an engaged one. Users started posting memes and similar videos, generating more buzz. Xiaomi had mastered the art of using seemingly inane stunts to go viral.

In an interesting TED Talk, Dao Nguyen, a publisher at the digital media platform BuzzFeed, broke down some of the ways BuzzFeed had managed to regularly deliver viral videos.[15] Dao described an instance where some of the company's employees had decided to prank their boss on his birthday. As part of the

---

15 https://www.youtube.com/watch?v=Kab-mpU-YVM

surprise, the team left some baby goats in his office and then decided to livestream the entire event on Facebook. What was initially planned as an inside joke for the rest of the office crew soon caught the notice of Facebook's regular users who happened to chance upon the livestream and then stuck around to watch as the story unfolded. In thirty minutes, as many as 90,000 viewers were watching the livestream. Dao said that when the team sat down to dissect what worked in favour of the video, they realized that those watching the video were excited 'because they were participating in the shared anticipation of something that was about to happen. They were part of a community, just for an instant, and it made them happy.'[16] This is the same logic that helped the video of the box brothers (as they came to be called) become a viral sensation. In this case, the video first got the viewers hooked to the theatrics of two full-bodied people jostling for space on top of a tiny packaging box. By the end of the video, viewers came out with a wholesome experience, but they were also playfully educated about the sturdiness of Xiaomi's packaging boxes. In short, it got the information across without sounding preachy.

Xiaomi fans also come with other benefits to the company. Many times even rescuing the company from embarrassment and sometimes passionately arguing to defend products subject to critique. On his first major product launch in India in 2015, the ever-so-charismatic Lei struggled with English. While he stumbled on several occasions, one particular phrase was subject to ridicule on the interwebs. After whipping up a frenzy about the new phone, instead of asking the audience, 'Are you excited?'

16 Ibid.

Lei ended up asking them, 'Are you okay?' many times on the stage. The video was uploaded on China's microblogging site Weibo, and many people (purportedly instigated by rivals) derided Lei's diction. A video uploaded on Youku racked up over 440,000 views in twenty-four hours.[17] Xiaomi fans jumped into action and vehemently defended Lei and praised him for his confidence. At a press conference in Bengaluru, which this writer also attended, and subsequent press briefings on the trip, Lei stuck to speaking in Chinese and used a translator to get his message across. To his credit, Lei, who made his billions despite not being a smooth English speaker, was playful and honest in his response. 'In China's education system, we actually studied English from middle school all the way through college,' he told the *Wall Street Journal*. 'My English test scores were all very good, but it turns out it was only very good in the tests,' he said.[18] A Xiaomi employee, on condition of anonymity, later said that Xiaomi's public relations team also quickly jumped into action and spun the story around. They seeded memes and, fun videos, and with the help of Mi Fans, made it a largely positive and wildly popular event. Xiaomi also has unofficial groups on Telegram where employees nudge fans to debunk critical reviews of its products.

The strategy of promoting via WeMedia was a huge success. By mid 2014, there were 20 million users on Xiaomi's BBSs, 30 million on QZone and upwards of 6 million on both Weibo and WeChat. In 2016, Li Wanqiang claimed that over 2 million

---

17 https://blogs.wsj.com/chinarealtime/2015/04/28/are-you-ok-xiaomi-
    ceos-awkward-english-goes-viral-sparks-debate/

18 Ibid.

visitors accessed the BBSs every day and that daily participation is over 300,000, which is ten times that of similar firms'. As an internet company, Xiaomi was using the right channels to spread the good word about its products. Remember how Xiaomi had been against the use of traditional advertising—the mantra that said, 'don't create ads; create good content'? It has put this theory into practice and regularly posts good content on WeMedia platforms. Since the posts are relatable and prioritize the user, they are liked and shared organically by users, which creates buzz around the brand.

But not all activities are restricted to digital platforms. As users turned into avid fans, Xiaomi started hosting gala events to generate enthusiasm about Xiaomi as a brand. The company has a large following among the youth, and it decided to tap into the community with great success. The elaborate shindig known as Mi Pop brings Mi Fans from around the country together to participate in fun games, live demos and general meet and greets.[19] Fans get a chance to meet top Xiaomi executives and click selfies with them. Registered attendees get free Mi t-shirts and other freebies. Mascots, phones and other accessories are available for sale, and the whole event receives live coverage from fans, many of whom are also video bloggers. Just like the digital activities on Xiaomi's WeMedia pages, these events serve two important functions—first, they turn users into spokespeople of the brand. Second, since the recommendation comes from actual users and not as a part of the company's paid campaigns, it has an authentic ring to it

---

19 https://c.mi.com/bd/forum-2376-1.html

and convinces new users to buy Xiaomi products in a way no traditional promotions can.

Apart from Mi Pop, a few hundred lucky fans also get to hang out with Lei and others during New Year's Eve every year at the company's headquarters. Reportedly, every year 'hundreds of Mi Fans from all over the world are invited to Xiaomi's headquarters, where executives, including Lei, cook for them and celebrate the New Year together'.[20]

Hiring Mi Fans as employees

That is not all. From its early days, Lei had realized the power of Mi Fans and wanted to channel this enthusiasm into Xiaomi's central workforce. He instructed offices to proactively recruit Mi Fans as Xiaomi employees. At the time of writing this chapter, for instance, Xiaomi India has over twenty employees hired from the fan community. As a report in the Indian daily, the *Hindu* read, Xiaomi has successfully cracked the code on 'Turning product fans into passionate employees'. Take Bhavya Maniar, for example. Bhavya was a beta tester for the company during his days at engineering college. Once he graduated, he formally joined Xiaomi as a marketing executive. There are many more like Bhavya. Unlike regular employees who take longer to create a personal attachment to the company they are serving, fans bring an incredible amount of passion and motivation to the table from day one.[21]

As for others who have not been directly incorporated into Xiaomi, the company makes sure such users, indeed the majority

---

20 https://www.borderless.net/news/borderlessfuture/making-technology-accessible-to-everyone-everywhere/

21 https://www.thehindubusinessline.com/specials/people-at-work/turning-product-fans-into-passionate-employees/article30685759.ece

of them, feel important along the way. The social media team at Xiaomi routinely comes up with novel ways to make fans feel like they are an integral part of the community. They host contests and feature the best photo entries on Xiaomi's social media page on a regular basis. The contests bring greater user engagement, and the photos illustrate the hi-spec features of Mi phone cameras while validating the photography skills of its user base. On 23 July 2019, Manu Jain tweeted '#MiTurns5: 5 incredible years for @XiaomiIndia! India's most loved brand. As I reflect back, I see the Mi Fan in me growing stronger. I'm celebrating by changing my name to "#MiFan Manu Kumar Jain." If you too are a true Mi Fan, do prefix #MiFan to your name!' Thousands of Mi Fans used the hashtag before their name as part of their Twitter handle. This continued for months on end. The #MiFan prefix reduced the distance between a top executive at a global corporation and regular users. In that given moment, regardless of how different their lives were, they all became one—diehard Mi Fans. It also showed the power of a brand that could attach itself so effortlessly to someone's virtual identity. Jessie Paul, the author of *No Money Marketing* says:

'Xiaomi is following a classical challenger's playbook. They have a good product at an attractive price. A clearly defined audience that is not core to their key competitors. An outreach program based on a pull strategy along with a nurture campaign for a B2C audience. Using online and flash sales as their primary sales tool in the early years.'

Jain and a few top leaders are anointed as key opinion leaders at Xiaomi. Unlike traditional brands that do not spend money to build up individuals and their social profiles, Xiaomi spends time and resources in building up their key opinion leaders. The idea is simple. Instead of having to go through influencers, the media or buy expensive advertising, build up your key opinion leaders, build a direct relationship with your audience and own the narrative. A quick analysis of Jain's Twitter page on WayBackMachine shows that in July 2014, he had only 448 followers. By May 2015, this had grown to 5,942 followers. He had 15,800 followers in July 2016, and by April 2018, his followers had grown more than tenfold to 164,000. By November 2020, his Twitter follower count had grown to over 422,900, making him one of the most influential voices on Twitter. On LinkedIn and other platforms, he has grown his followers to reach millions of people.

In 2019, after completing five successful years in India, Xiaomi released a short celebratory video featuring several Mi Fans. It showcased different Mi products and reminded viewers of the many milestones that Xiaomi India had reached in such a short time. The video was titled 'No Mi Without You', which is perhaps one of the most fitting and self-reflective brand promotions to have come out in recent times.[22] The branding team at Xiaomi put it better than all its reviewers and critics combined—there indeed is no Mi without its users.

Honest pricing

Memes and superfans are great. But it would be a disservice to years of research on pricing if we don't look at the role Xiaomi's 'honest pricing' strategy has played in making it a loved brand. In 2011, at the time of launching its first device, Lei told his

22 https://www.campaignindia.in/video/xiaomi-celebrates-five-year-journey-in-india-by-thanking-consumers-says-nomiwit/453450

employees that he wanted to build a phone that performs better than a $600 phone but retails at only $300. This meant forgoing margins—a taboo in the manufacturing industry. But Lei is more than okay with that. Back in the nineties at Kingsoft, Lei had made the unprecedented move of launching its antivirus software for free when it was unfathomable to do so. In later years, internet companies have never flinched at the thought of losing money to acquire users. In fact, this is one of the levers many Silicon Valley companies have used to successfully take down incumbents. As we saw earlier, if you look at Xiaomi as an internet company, and not a smartphone maker, the economics make a lot more sense. Traditionally, internet companies spend money to acquire users. But in Xiaomi's case, it was getting paid as it acquired new users.

Xiaomi has stuck to its pricing strategy even today. For instance, the Mi 10 flagship series of 5G phones announced by Xiaomi in February 2020 has a bill of materials (cost of all components that go into the phone) of about $440, according to TechInsights.[23] But it is expected to retail at just under $700. That is a good deal cheaper than most other phones of similar specifications sold by Samsung or Apple. Of course, for customers who buy products to signal status, a play on pricing might not work. But for Xiaomi, which needs to have more and more users for its business model to work, volumes are more important than a relatively smaller number of premium users.

Back in 2018, at the time of listing, Lei did something even bolder. He wrote to prospective shareholders, 'At this point, I would like to pledge to our existing and potential users: starting in 2018, Xiaomi's hardware business' overall net profit margin

---

23 https://www.techinsights.com/blog/xiaomi-mi-10-teardown-analysis

will not exceed 5% per year. If the net margin exceeds 5%, we will return the excess to our users.'[24] This not only demonstrated Xiaomi's commitment to its users and showed how products from competitors were overpriced, but also forced Xiaomi to think of revenue and profits from services built on top of the Xiaomi platform and not just by marking up prices on hardware. The message was clear: Xiaomi is not a hardware company. It is an internet company, and that's how the company will unlock long-term value from its users. In its prospectus, it said, 'Xiaomi is an internet company with smartphones and smart hardware connected by an IoT [internet of things] platform at its core.'

Xiaomi calls it the triathlon business model. Imagine a triangle with the three corners as hardware, internet services, and e-commerce and new retail. The user is placed at the centre. Besides smartphones, Xiaomi sells smart TVs, fitness bands and a variety of smart devices under the IoT and lifestyle category. To retail these devices, Xiaomi has taken an omnichannel approach—that is, a combination of online and offline retail. By way of internet services, Xiaomi has the Android-based MIUI operating system, on top of which it has apps such as the Mi App Store, Mi Browser, Mi Music and Mi Video. It also includes online gaming, e-commerce (Youpin), consumer finance and television internet services in its internet services business. 'Compared to other internet platforms that acquire new users at high costs, we leverage the sale of our hardware to acquire users at a profit,' the Xiaomi prospectus said.

---

24 http://blog.mi.com/en/2018/04/25/xiaomis-hardware-business-will-have-an-overall-net-profit-margin-that-will-never-exceed-5-percent/

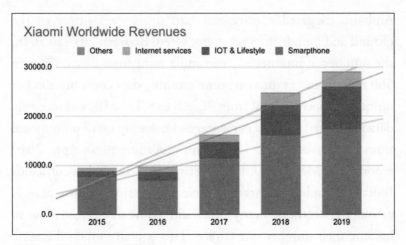

Source: Company Filings.

To borrow an oft used phrase coined by the late management guru Clay Christensen, Xiaomi is a classic 'disruptive innovator'. Disruptive innovations aren't usually the best in class when introduced. However, as Christensen notes in his paper, they offer a 'novel mix of attributes that appeals to fringe customer groups, notably those near the bottom of the market. They may be, for instance, smaller, cheaper, more accessible, or more convenient.'[25] Clearly, Xiaomi chose to make its phones cheaper and go after the bottom of the market as a strategy, and it paid off. In markets such as India, when millions of users started to buy smartphones thanks to cheap data, better connectivity and compelling content, Xiaomi was there with the right value proposition: the most affordable flagship phones you can buy. The 2015 launch of Jio, the telecom company bankrolled by India's richest man Mukesh

---

25 https://www.researchgate.net/publication/325803847_Disruptive_Innovation_An_Intellectual_History_and_Directions_for_Future_Research

Ambani, triggered a price war and drove data prices to the ground and mobile internet skyrocketed. Between 2014 to 2018, the number of internet users in India went from 239 million to 560 million and at the same time monthly data consumption per unique connection went from 86 MB to 8,320 MB, and monthly data price per 1 GB as a percentage of monthly GDP plummeted from 6.1 per cent to 0.1 per cent, according to an April 2019 report from McKinsey Global Institute.[26] When value-conscious Indians thought of upgrading their phones from feature phones or older-generation smartphones, the affordably-priced Xiaomi became their number one choice. This is pretty much the same way it worked for Xiaomi in China during the years its middle class grew.

Yet another aspect Christensen points out about disruptive innovators is:

'Existing customers and established profit models constrain established firms' investments in new innovations; thus, investments unattractive to incumbents may be attractive to entrants who lack many (or any) customers and enjoy fewer competing investment opportunities. Consequently, incumbents are typically unmotivated to develop disruptive innovations that promise lower margins, target smaller markets and introduce inferior products and services that their existing customers cannot use.'

---

26 https://www.mckinsey.com/~/media/McKinsey/Business%20Functions/
McKinsey%20Digital/Our%20Insights/Digital%20India%20
Technology%20to%20transform%20a%20connected%20nation/MGI-
Digital-India-Report-April-2019.ashx

In Xiaomi's case, competitors were not only constrained by their profit models, which were built to distribute the devices using expensive marketing and layers of offline retailers, but also by huge technical debts. Xiaomi, which started with a clean slate, could afford to sell online, focus on rapid product development and eschew expensive marketing. Thus, it became a disruptor in an industry where incumbents were too slow to respond.

In 2019, however, Xiaomi tweaked its strategy to reflect new realities. The company officially launched its 'smartphones + AIoT' dual-engine strategy. The idea, according to Lei's letter to shareholders, is to strengthen processes and invest in innovation, quality control and supply chain management; as well as promote their multi-brand strategy in their smartphone business. The second engine would be Xiaomi's AIoT (Artificial Intelligence of Things) platform, where it hopes to marry the internet of things and AI. To that end, the company committed to investing RMB 10 billion over the next five years in AIoT. As of December 2018, Xiaomi had over 150.9 million units (excluding smartphones) connected to its platform. The company also tied up with Ikea to connect a set of smart lighting solutions to Xiaomi's IoT platform.[27] This gives Xiaomi enough and more data to experiment and push the boundaries of AI. With its focus on IoT and AI, Xiaomi has opened up two new frontiers for the company. Both are large and rapidly evolving markets, effectively increasing Xiaomi's total addressable market multifold. This is something market watchers who narrowly focus on the smartphone industry often miss out about Xiaomi. Once Xiaomi sells a phone to a user or a fan, it

---

27 http://blog.mi.com/en/2018/11/28/news-xiaomi-and-ikea-partner-to-bring-smart-connected-homes-to-more-users/

easily expands its footprint into other areas because the user has already experienced Xiaomi. For instance, after putting credible smartphones in your hands, Xiaomi has moved on to your living room with smart TVs and air purifiers; to your bathroom with electric toothbrushes and smart scales; to your gym and to outdoors with their fitness bands; and to your workplace with their laptops. It also sells security cameras, soap dispensers, battery packs, earphones and many other accessories, thanks to its ability to quickly identify within its user groups the products it should launch next. The company has over 200 products in its portfolio that it has developed through 'ecosystem partners'. The idea is to connect all of them through its IoT platform and use that data to further launch AI-powered products. In India, many of these products have been successful. When I met Xiaomi India's chief business officer (then head of online sales) Raghu Reddy in early 2019, the company had already become the largest seller of wearable bands and smart TVs in India. In the first quarter of 2020, Xiaomi maintained its lead with a 27 per cent share of India's smart TV market followed by incumbents such as LG and Samsung at 14 per cent and 10 per cent respectively.[28] According to Counterpoint Research, on the back of rising demand for streaming content (think big league cricket matches on Hotstar and binge-worthy serials on Netflix and Amazon Prime), a record 15 million smart TVs were sold in India in 2019.[29] More than 200 million households in India have TV sets, and the market for smart TVs is big. 'This growth is mainly driven by budget smart

---

28 https://www.newindianexpress.com/business/2020/jun/18/smartphone-players-rise-in-india-smart-tv-market-xiaomi-leads-2158172.html

29 https://www.counterpointresearch.com/india-tv-shipments-climb-record-15-million-units-2019-15-annually/

TVs with 32-inch TVs leading the segment and penetrating sub-US$150 price bands,' the market research firm noted. Xiaomi's 32-inch smart TVs sell for about ₹12,499 or about $167. Similarly, in the wearable's category, Xiaomi's bands, which sell for between ₹1,299 and ₹2,299 ($17.4 to $30.8), lead in sales with 5.3 million devices sold in 2019. That's a growth of over 50 per cent over the previous year and a market share of 49 per cent. Titan, India's largest watch brand, had a 14.5 per cent market share in smart watches.[30]

There are many parallels to this strategy (a combination of aggressive pricing and multiple products) in other industries. In one sense, it's the classic 'land and expand strategy' perfected by software companies. Software companies often allow users to try their products for free or at a nominal cost, making it easy for sales and marketing teams to land a customer. Eventually, they grow their wallet share with the customer by selling them premium features (with the freemium model), newer products (with the multi-product model) or more licences, thereby expanding their relationship with the customer. If you rewind a little further, the widely studied Razorblade model of consumer goods company Gillette comes to mind. The strategy is to sell a product (in this case, the phone) at very little or no margins and sell consumables that are essential for that product to function. The consumables generate reliable, recurring revenue, and the original product keeps the user locked to a platform. In the case of Xiaomi, the smartphone is just the gateway to the user. Further down the road, it sells your attention to the highest bidder through its

---

30 https://www.idc.com/getdoc.jsp?containerId=prAP46093320

advertising platform and also several other goods like mobile phone accessories and services such as financial credit.

Not everyone is sold on Xiaomi's strategy to make money off software and services. 'Long-term, Xiaomi's biggest problem will be trying to make money on smartphones and other smart devices instead of services. They have sold smart devices at a very small gross profit with the idea that they will one day make money on software and services. This does not appear to be happening, and they will have to eventually accept that they are a handset maker, not an internet company,' says Jeffery Towson, private equity investor and professor at Peking University. Data bears out Towson's views. As you can see from the chart on page 149, even though Xiaomi's advertising revenues have grown at a healthy clip over the years, as a percentage of its revenues in 2019, advertising is still at 9.6 per cent, a number that it had achieved in 2016. Meanwhile, revenue percentage from smartphones has gone down from 71.3 per cent in 2016 to 59.3 per cent, and IoT and lifestyle products have grown from 18.1 per cent in 2016 to 30.2 per cent in 2019 as a percentage of revenues. Total revenues at the end of 2019 stood at RMB 205.84 billion ($29.25 billion).[31]

---

31 Annual results announcement for the year ended 31 December 2019. Xiaomi Corporation.

Chapter 6
Next is What?

IT WAS ANDY GROVE, one of the most successful chief executives of corporate America, who said that a corporation is a living organism. 'Methods have to change. Focus has to change. Values have to change. The sum total of those changes is transformation,' Grove, the founder and CEO of Intel Inc., said.[1] The need for this evolution comes from his understanding that 'only the paranoid survive'. Xiaomi's user-centric approach gives it superpowers that many of its competitors do not have. The company, though no longer a start-up, is still nimble and geared to quickly adapt, change and transform itself based on its users' needs. These are indeed superpowers in today's hyper-competitive business landscape. Yet, every superhero has their Kryptonite.

---

1   https://www.esquire.com/entertainment/interviews/a1449/learned-andy-grove-0500/

We have witnessed Xiaomi's rise from the dreams and meticulous planning of its chief founder, Lei Jun. We have also seen how the company exploded onto the scene thanks to Lei's prescience about the 2010s being the decade of the internet and the rise of social media that helped newer brands reach their customers. Over time, Xiaomi became one of the most loved brands in China and even had its fair share of success globally. But the most colourful feather in its cap has undoubtedly been India, where it toppled Samsung and became the number one smartphone seller in just four years. Which brings us to the question, next is what? It is the tagline that Samsung used in its ads in 2008-09, and it seems fitting that we end this book borrowing Samsung's mantra to understand what the future really holds for Xiaomi. In the Indian version of a Samsung advertisement featuring Bollywood superstar Aamir Khan, the voiceover asks, 'What is the next thing I have got to do to better myself?' as Khan stares sharply back at you through the screen and from billboards.[2] As Xiaomi completes ten years, the question we should all be asking is what is the next thing Xiaomi is planning to stay ahead in the race. But also, and perhaps more importantly, the question we should really be asking is, are there any stumbling blocks that might cost Xiaomi dearly in the long run? It's hard to predict the future and hence harder to pinpoint what Xiaomi's Kryptonite could be. So we'll limit this chapter to an exploration of some of the larger trends that are playing out in the market.

We began this book with the rise of Xiaomi. But as it happens with the rise and fall of empires, Xiaomi rose to the top as Nokia

---

2   https://www.youtube.com/watch?v=qPvn_aK8ReA

and Motorola fell after they failed to quickly transition to the smartphone era. To paraphrase poet T. S. Eliot, their world ended not with a bang but a whimper. As the Finnish and American companies quietly vacated the scene, the Chinese took centre stage. Not just Xiaomi, China has given the world some of the most popular brands in the past few years. From OnePlus to Oppo, Vivo and now Realme, the current smartphone market is largely the stage for Chinese enterprises. This has had far-reaching implications for Xiaomi as a brand. One of the key ambitions of Lei, as we have repeatedly mentioned in this book, is to destigmatize China's reputation as the land of cheap labour and cheaper products. Now that it has been fulfilled and credible Chinese products have come to flood the global market, we need to understand what effect this has had or may have in the future for Xiaomi as a brand. How, for instance, does Xiaomi plan on holding its position in the face of increasing competition? Moreover, what has Xiaomi learnt from brands that quickly shot to popularity but were even quicker to meet with failures and rendered irrelevant?

We have already discussed how Nokia and Motorola became obsolete in the early 2010s, but there is another brand that deserves mention here. In 2009, the company Research In Motion (RIM) was ranked at the top of its list of 199 fastest-growing companies in the world by *Fortune* magazine.[3] For those who are too young to remember, RIM was the maker of the iconic BlackBerry smartphones. Rod McQueen notes in his book, *BlackBerry: The Inside Story of Research In Motion,* that at

---

3   https://archive.fortune.com/2009/08/12/technology/blackberry_research_in_motion.fortune/index.htm

the time RIM had already become Canada's most valuable tech company with annual revenues approaching $15 billion and an eye-popping five-year revenue growth rate of 910 per cent. Much like Xiaomi's growth has been powered by the macro trend of participatory consumption, BlackBerry's rise was buoyed by the first wave of consumerization of enterprise technology. The US telephony market opened up and grew quickly in the eighties and the nineties. After the break-up of AT&T, and Motorola's innovations with the handheld radio that gave birth to the first commercial mobile phone, mobile telephony became popular. But the concept of mobile internet was still new. The mobile phone market was dominated by Motorola, Ericsson, Nokia and Siemens. Soon, Samsung replaced Siemens and then RIM entered the scene with a brand-new feature—push emails, which meant users were now always connected to their email on their mobile phones.

The coming together of the mobile phone and email and the need for enterprise users to be constantly logged into their email accounts were what powered BlackBerry's rise in the early days. Soon, as BlackBerry became more and more consumer-friendly with offerings like the BlackBerry messenger, it broke out of the enterprise world and established itself as a popular consumer electronic device. The rise of RIM is illustrative of how technology shifts can turn relatively unknown and niche upstarts into globally successful giants.

But the launch of the iPhone in 2007 and later the launch of commercial Android devices in 2008 had already set the wheels in motion for an upheaval in the smartphone industry. In less than ten years, RIM went from being a celebrated tech company with deep engineering prowess and considerable market share to a nobody in the smartphone business. In 2011, BlackBerry had to lay off 2,000 employees.[4] In January 2012, the company's illustrious co-CEOs, Mike Lazaridis and Jim Balsillie, had to quit.[5] In 2013, the number of active BlackBerry subscribers started shrinking and sales started nosediving, dragging its topline down and making it an unprofitable company. No doubt BlackBerry was an innovator, but it failed to keep up with the times, or rather users.

BlackBerry's run as a smartphone company had come to an end along with hundreds of other companies that couldn't manage the transition to the smartphone era.

'BlackBerry's failure to keep up with Apple and Google was a consequence of errors in its strategy and vision. First, after growing to dominate the corporate market, BlackBerry failed to anticipate that consumers—not business customers—would drive the smartphone revolution. Second, BlackBerry was blindsided by the emergence of the "app economy," which drove massive adoption of iPhone and Android-based devices. Third, BlackBerry failed to realize that smartphones would evolve beyond mere communication devices to become full-fledged mobile entertainment hubs.'

---

4   https://www.wsj.com/articles/SB10001424053111903591104576467711532275104

5   https://www.nytimes.com/2012/01/23/technology/rims-jim-balsillie-and-mike-lazaridis-step-aside.html

Sam Gustin wrote about BlackBerry's failure in *Time* magazine.[6] The history of telecommunications is replete with companies that died because they couldn't keep pace with changing times. A decade can be a long time in the business of smartphones, and lasting success is never a given. Many other companies, pioneers in their own right, were also crushed by the smartphone revolution. Xiaomi's fate could be different. But it could also be the same. For Xiaomi, which has defied all odds until now, there are a few headwinds.

The battle of nations

Meng Wanzhou, chief financial officer (CFO) of Huawei, China's biggest privately held company, was in for a rude shock when she landed in Vancouver, Canada, on 1 December 2018. She was arrested at the behest of US authorities. Forty-eight-year-old Meng was no ordinary CFO: she is the daughter of Huawei founder Ren Zhengfei. Huawei reported revenues of $122 billion in 2019. Meng was accused of covering up Huawei activities that violated US sanctions on Iran. This was a low point in trade relations between the US and China.

The mounting tensions between China and the US do not concern Xiaomi directly, not yet anyway, but they do concern Chinese firms in general and Huawei in particular. Huawei, which started in 1987 in Shenzhen, China's first SEZ, is not only the largest telecom equipment company in the world but also one of the leading smartphone brands. Its founder Ren was a former engineer of the People's Liberation Army in China. His

---

6   https://business.time.com/2013/09/24/the-fatal-mistake-that-doomed-blackberry/

military past and close connections with the Chinese Communist Party became a matter of great contention once it came to be widely believed that business with Huawei could potentially be a breach of national security. From early 2012, the US government had suspected Huawei of sharing intelligence with the Chinese government. Ever since then, America's relations with China have been fraught with tension, but the matter escalated significantly once Donald Trump was elected president of the US in 2016 and US–China trade relations took an ugly turn. In 2018, the director of the Federal Bureau of Investigation (FBI), Christopher Wray, was reported as saying, 'We're deeply concerned about the risks of allowing any company or entity that is beholden to foreign governments that don't share our values to gain positions of power inside our telecommunications networks that provides the capacity to exert pressure or control over our telecommunications infrastructure.'[7] Following this, the Pentagon banned the use of Huawei devices in US military bases. This was seen as a measure to stop 'Chinese spies' from eavesdropping on sensitive US communication.

In April 2019, Bloomberg, citing confidential sources, reported that it found security holes in the internet routers supplied by Huawei, raising suspicion that the Chinese supplier was enabling eavesdropping.[8] Vodafone also found vulnerabilities in some of its optic fibre network set up by Huawei. Bloomberg reported that Huawei is banned in Australia, Japan, Taiwan and the US, economies that together make up nearly a third of the

---

7   https://www.cnbc.com/2018/02/13/chinas-hauwei-top-us-intelligence-
    chiefs-caution-americans-away.html

8   https://www.bloomberg.com/news/articles/2019-04-30/vodafone-
    found-hidden-backdoors-in-huawei-equipment

global GDP. The list of countries in which Huawei is banned is only growing.

Both Huawei and Vodafone issued rebuttals. Huawei said, 'The story published by Bloomberg today is misleading. It refers to a maintenance and diagnostic function, common across the industry, as well as vulnerabilities, which were corrected over seven years ago. There is absolutely no truth in the suggestion that Huawei conceals backdoors in its equipment.'[9]

A spokesman for Vodafone said, 'The "backdoor" that Bloomberg refers to is telnet, which is a protocol that is commonly used by many vendors in the industry for performing diagnostic functions. It would not have been accessible from the internet.'[10] Bloomberg is incorrect in saying that this 'could have given Huawei unauthorised access to the carrier's fixed-line network in Italy'. Vodafone also said it had not found evidence of any unauthorized access.

Huawei has consistently denied these allegations. To the allegation of close ties with the Chinese military, Tian Tao, a member of Huawei's international advisory council, and Wu Chunbo of Renmin University wrote in the book *The Huawei Story* that Ren's military past is no different from that of scores of CEOs of Fortune 500 companies who have previously worked for the US armed forces. Huawei also said that it had hired US-based consulting firm KPMG for over a decade to audit its financial statements and dared its detractors to find evidence of the alleged financial support it received from the Chinese government. All

---

9   https://www.theguardian.com/technology/2019/apr/30/alleged-huawei-router-backdoor-is-standard-networking-tool-says-firm

10   https://www.bbc.com/news/business-48103430

this, however, did not stop American lawmakers from preventing Huawei from buying into American companies such as 3Com and the wireless business of Motorola.

In November 2018, US President Donald Trump and China's President Xi Jinping met at the G20 summit in Barcelona and decided to bury the hatchet. Unlike Nixon's 1972 visit to China, Trump's meeting with Xi did not result in better relations between the two countries. Only days after this 'peace pact', Meng was detained in Vancouver. Vox described this as a 'warning shot' to US–China relations, suggesting that despite the diplomatic agreement in Barcelona between Xi and Trump, the trade war between the two countries was far from over.[11] Huawei, on its part, responded to the incident via an official tweet claiming that Meng's extradition was based on 'unspecified charges'. As it turns out, the US had been investigating Huawei for a long time, and the CFO's arrest was a consequence of alleged violations of US sanctions in Iran. In January 2019, US federal prosecutors officially charged Meng and Huawei with bank and wire fraud and with allegations of defrauding the US and stealing confidential data. This was just the tip of the iceberg. The FBI is looking into over a thousand cases of alleged (IP) theft— ranging from cutting edge research at universities to industrial technologies—involving Chinese companies and individuals.[12]

Following the arrest of Meng in December 2018, in May 2019, the Trump administration barred American companies from using information and communication technology of *any*

11 https://www.vox.com/policy-and-politics/2018/12/6/18128900/huawei-sabrina-meng-arrest-canada-china-us

12 https://www.zdnet.com/article/fbi-is-investigating-more-than-1000-cases-of-chinese-theft-of-us-technology/

company that could be a threat to its national security. This was deemed a matter of national emergency, and even though no company was explicitly named in the executive order, everyone knew it was Huawei that Trump was going after. In fact, if it was not clear before, that very day the US government released an 'entity list', a blacklist that effectively barred Huawei and its seventy affiliates from carrying on business with the US without the government's approval.[13] Following orders, many US companies thought it best to rescind their business ties with Huawei. Everyone agreed that Huawei products were of great quality. But at the same time, no one could conclusively prove that allegations regarding the company's involvement in Chinese intelligence services were false. In terms of actual impact, the restriction meant that US companies such as Google and Intel were barred from doing business with Huawei unless they received a government licence to do so.

The narrative now shifted from what Huawei had *already* done to what it could *potentially* do to America in the future. In November 2019, CNN did an exclusive interview with Ren to find out how Huawei was going to operate in the future now that it could no longer do business with Google. Unperturbed by the question and the insurmountable pressure Huawei must have been feeling at the time, Ren smilingly responded that he was confident that with time Huawei was going to become the number one telecom brand with or without Google's help. At the time Huawei was blacklisted, it was only second in line to being the world's most popular smartphone vendor; Samsung was on

---

13 https://www.reuters.com/article/us-usa-china-huaweitech/chinas-huawei-70-affiliates-placed-on-us-trade-blacklist-idUSKCN1SL2W4

top of the list. Ren replied, 'I don't think that'll be a problem; it just takes time.' The interviewer pressed him, 'Takes time? How are you going to crack into the overseas market without Google?' Ren again clarified, 'When I say it takes time, what I am referring to is the overseas market. Because we will return to the overseas market next year and the year after that. We have full capability and determination.'[14]

As it happens, the company had already been investing billions of dollars in research and development. In 2018, much before it got blacklisted in the US, Huawei had increased its annual R&D budget from $15 billion to $20 billion.[15] Huawei had also been working on developing its own operating system, Harmony, and even though it only had 45,000 apps available on it at the time compared to 2.8 million on the Google Play Store, it was certain that with time, it could surpass that number. The company is also developing its own mobile chipsets.

Huawei's predicament has had two very important implications for Chinese firms such as Xiaomi. On the one hand, the trade war has rendered them vulnerable in the overseas market, especially in the US, which Xiaomi has been planning to enter for a long time, without success. But on the other hand, it has shown the resilience of Huawei to stand tall in the face of great adversity, thus reinforcing the old saying: what doesn't kill you only makes you stronger. Broadly speaking, Huawei's troubles in the US can be instructive to other Chinese companies such as Xiaomi.

---

14 https://edition.cnn.com/videos/business/2019/11/26/huawei-smartphone-ren-zhenfei-google-stout-vpx.cnn

15 https://www.scmp.com/tech/social-gadgets/article/2157024/huawei-raise-minimum-annual-rd-spending-least-us15-billion

Patent troubles ahead

Besides geopolitical risks that threaten business relationships, Xiaomi's patent problem is also a challenge. In 2018, when Xiaomi published its IPO prospectus, one of the chief risks it listed was Xiaomi being repeatedly charged with infringement of property rights by several companies. It openly stated,

> 'In particular, we have been, and may continue to be, subject to various intellectual property claims, including patent, copyright and trademark disputes, relating to technologies or intellectual property used in our products and services and claiming infringement or violations of intellectual property rights and new claims may arise in the future.'[16]

In fact, in 2014, Ericsson had charged Xiaomi India of infringing eight of its patents registered in India without procuring a valid licence from Ericsson. The two companies agreed on a licensing deal and settled the litigation outside the courts. In 2018, TOT Power Control SL similarly alleged that Xiaomi had infringed one of its patents registered in Spain. That same year, Yulong Computer Telecommunication Scientific Co. took Xiaomi to court in Shenzhen for infringing three of its patents. Xiaomi has had many such cases of infringing content and services, and as the prospectus stated, it is difficult to say that such instances will not occur in the future.

---

16 The Xiaomi Prospectus.

To be sure, Xiaomi has been increasing its investments in R&D lately. Between 2016 and 2019, the company's R&D expenses grew at a compound annual growth rate of 53 per cent. In 2016, for instance, it spent only about RMB 2.1 billion on R&D. In 2020, it expects to spend five times more on R&D, the company said in March 2020 during the announcement of its financial results.

Xiaomi's patent problems are largely an outcome of how it conducts its business. The company is committed to introducing new and 'explosive' products at regular intervals and transitioning to improved technology at a quick pace to survive competition from other brands and satisfy user demands. This constant focus on launching new products and keeping the users engaged has continued to come in the way of Xiaomi trying to build a defensible patent portfolio. For the most part, Xiaomi relies on access to third-party IP. Getting a licence from these third parties often takes time and costs money, not to mention the impact it has on the products' profitability. If Xiaomi wishes to make its patent problems go away and stay ahead in the competition, it will probably have to adopt a new strategy that allows it to build a robust patent portfolio without compromising its broader business goals.

As the US–China trade war intensifies, America will bring to bear everything at its disposal, including patent laws, to block Chinese companies from selling in the market. Xiaomi's patent portfolio, as is widely known, is quite weak. Huawei, on the other hand, has steadily grown its patent portfolio, becoming the first Chinese company to top the list of patent applications worldwide in 2008.[17] These were not exactly smartphone-related patents, but a portfolio of patents comes in handy when negotiating deals and warding off litigants in the telecommunications sector. The problem is explained well in the book *The Huawei Story*: The company paid $222 million in patent royalties and over $600 million to Qualcomm to earn contracts worth over $20 billion. One quote by Ren in the book is particularly telling:

> 'Huawei has managed to carry its banner uphill and planted it on the top. But then it finds out that it has been surrounded by its enemies. Virtually all essential patents in the telecom industry belong to Western companies. After 10 years of technology accumulation, Huawei has been caught in an unpleasant situation: yes, it is on top of the hill, but it has been barricaded by enemies who occupy the foot of the hill and the hillside.'[18]

The smartphone industry is no different from the larger telecom industry when it comes to patents. RPX, a patent risk-management firm, claims that today over 250,000 US patents are applicable to a smartphone.[19] Of this, a big chunk goes to companies such as Qualcomm that own critical patents. Sample this: In the fiscal year 2019, San Diego-based Qualcomm Inc. reported total revenues of $24.3 billion.[20] In the year before that, it made $22.6 billion. Of this, nearly 10 per cent came from

---

17 *The Huawei Story*, op. citation.

18 Ibid.

19 Li Wanqiang, *The Xiaomi Way*, op. cit.

20 https://www.qualcomm.com/news/releases/2019/11/06/qualcomm-announces-fourth-quarter-and-fiscal-2019-results

Xiaomi, according to company filings.[21] This means Xiaomi paid Qualcomm upwards of \$4.5 billion in two years for its chipsets and as licensing fees. Little wonder that Ericsson didn't want Xiaomi selling phones with unlicensed chips in India. A teardown of Xiaomi's devices will show that most major chips used are from Qualcomm. If things take a more serious turn, Washington could not only shut its doors to Chinese companies but also issue diktats to prevent American companies like Qualcomm Inc. from selling to Chinese companies. Qualcomm points out this risk in its 2019 annual report.

> '… certain of our Chinese OEM customers have developed, and others may in the future develop their own integrated circuit products and use such integrated circuit products, or other integrated circuit products, in their devices rather than our integrated circuit products, whether due to pressure from the Chinese government as part of its broader economic policies, the OEMs' concerns over losing access to our integrated circuit products as a result of US/Chinese trade tensions, or otherwise. Further, political actions, including trade and/or national security protection policies, or other actions by governments, have in the past, currently are and could in the future limit or prevent us from transacting business with certain of our customers, or limit or prevent certain of our customers from transacting business with us.'

---

21 Annual results announcement for the year ended 31 December 2019. Xiaomi Corporation.

A threat of this nature, if it comes to pass, will tip the scales in favour of Huawei and Samsung; companies that are increasingly making their own chipsets. Xiaomi has reportedly abandoned efforts to develop chips.

Competition from other Chinese brands

Patents are a problem but not usually life-threatening. Most patent disputes are settled out of court, and a deal agreeable to both parties is worked out. But a more pressing concern for Xiaomi is competition from within China. Xiaomi is no longer competing with multinational giants that do not understand the nuances of the Chinese market or are disadvantaged by the country's protectionist regime. Its competition includes the venerable Huawei and other home-grown brands such as Oppo and Vivo. What makes them fierce rivals is that the supply chain and ecosystem advantages that are available to Xiaomi are available to them as well. Of them, Huawei, which has consistently sold over 30 per cent of the phones in China in the recent past, is the toughest rival. Its fallout with the US government has forced it to look inwards at the Chinese market, and selling smartphones is how it is making up for slowing revenues from its telecom equipment business. Huawei, a company known for its hard-working employees and a customer-centric approach, became serious about the smartphone business only a little before Xiaomi. The first Android-based Huawei phone was unveiled in 2009 at the Mobile World Congress, only a year before Xiaomi was founded. Since then, it has steadily grown its presence in China as well as elsewhere around the world. With its Honor brand of phones, Huawei had a 40 per cent market share by the third quarter of 2019. Xiaomi, on the other hand, has struggled to defend its market share, which is not only under threat from Huawei but also from Oppo and Vivo. As the chart below shows, at its peak in the fourth quarter of 2017, Xiaomi had a 15 per cent market share as compared to Huawei's 20 per cent. But since then, it has lost market share significantly. In the fourth quarter of 2019, Xiaomi was at 9 per cent as opposed to Huawei's 35 per cent.

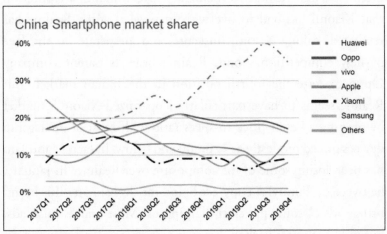

Source: Counterpoint Research.

In India, too, Xiaomi has had difficulties holding on to its number one position. In the second quarter of 2019, Xiaomi beat Samsung to become the number one smartphone vendor in India with a 28 per cent market share. Within months, the BBK group beat it at its game by capturing 30 per cent of the market. The BBK group is a Chinese multinational conglomerate that owns the popular smartphone brands Vivo, Oppo, Realme and OnePlus. 'What Xiaomi did to Apple and Samsung in China, other Chinese smartphone makers like Oppo and Vivo then did to them by entering with an even lower price,' said Towson of Peking University.

Realme especially has emerged as a true contender in recent times after it was touted as the fastest-growing smartphone brand in India in 2019. Realme climbed to the fifth position after showing a massive growth of over 263 per cent in 2019.[22] In a strange and rather ironic turn of events, Xiaomi officials have often criticized Realme for being a 'copycat' brand, a reputation that Xiaomi has had to live with for several years. Realme has retaliated, calling Xiaomi 'insecure' and 'desperate' in the face of new competition. Soon, Realme beat its parent company Oppo to seize the fourth position in the Indian market. But Realme seems to have particularly jeopardized Xiaomi's market by offering a better price-to-specs ratio with most of its flagship devices priced modestly at ₹20,000 and below. In fact, Manu Jain has been losing some of his composure over Realme. In January, he tweeted, 'Funny! A copy-cat brand mocks us. Later this brand brings ads & some ppl start blaming us. Most brands push ads, but only Xiaomi is bashed. Because we've been transparent about our business model. If any journalist wants to understand our internet business, I'm happy to talk!'

Competitive pricing, as we know, has been Xiaomi's trump card all along. Despite being ridiculed as the Apple copycat, Xiaomi managed to do so well because it offered great specs but at far better prices. Not only does Realme sound similar to Redmi, the name for Xiaomi's series phones, but also its better

---

22 https://www.livemint.com/technology/tech-news/realme-grew-at-
    massive-263-in-2019-but-xiaomi-growth-flat-11581074370730.html

pricing strategy might cost Xiaomi its precious, albeit price-sensitive fan/user base. Mass market users, especially in countries like India, tend to be value-conscious and do not bat an eyelid before switching over to a competing brand.

Remember the saying, what does not kill you only makes you stronger? In the face of extreme competition—both from Chinese and other international brands—Xiaomi has been able to stay afloat by adopting a different strategy. At the beginning of 2019, Lei announced that Xiaomi was going to invest $1.48 billion in smart products over the next five years. Xiaomi has always maintained that it was not merely a smartphone company, but rather an internet company. Over time, it expanded its product base to include smart TVs, water purifiers, air purifiers, rice cookers, a series of fitness wearables such as the Mi Band, and even a range of smart lighting solutions. There is little that Xiaomi does not sell today. However, it does not manufacture all these smart products by itself. Instead, it has outsourced the task of manufacturing them to smaller start-up enterprises that are funded by Xiaomi, which are then distributed under the Mi brand name. Xiaomi has thus created an ecosystem that has effectively increased its relevance in the lives of its fan-consumers, who have a whole line of products to choose from even when they are not thinking of purchasing a new Mi phone for themselves or their loved ones. At a time when new brands such as Realme are posing a challenge to Xiaomi's smartphone sector, its IoT-enabled products are allowing the company to compensate for the loss in smartphone market shares by cranking out newer products faster than before. As a percentage of revenues, Xiaomi's IoT and lifestyle products grew from 18.1 per cent in 2016 to 30.2 per cent in 2019.

#BoycottChina

No shots were fired, according to the government officials of India and China. But at least twenty Indian soldiers were killed as they clashed with Chinese soldiers in a disputed border area in June 2020. This was the first time in forty-five years that the two sides lost the lives of soldiers to conflict.[23] The conflict triggered latent anti-China sentiment in India, especially on social media, and hashtags such as #BoycottChina started trending. Several videos showing angry Indians destroying Chinese products and vowing to boycott Chinese goods surfaced in the days following the conflict. This spells more trouble for Chinese companies in India, including Xiaomi, which have made significant inroads into the Indian market in the past five to six years. In the days following the conflict, India banned more than 200 Chinese apps including popular apps such as TikTok and Helo, citing security reasons. India's ministry of information technology, under Section 69A of the Information Technology Act issued orders to block these apps and said in a press release dated 29 June 2020 that,

> 'they are engaged in activities which is prejudicial to sovereignty and integrity of India, defence of India, security of state and public order … This move will safeguard the interests of crores of Indian mobile and internet users. This decision is a targeted move to ensure safety and sovereignty of Indian cyberspace.'

---

23 https://www.bbc.com/news/world-asia-53061476

The move was praised by several Indian entrepreneurs, who see this as the beginning of India's bid to create a favourable environment for local companies and as an opportunity to grow without having to compete with Chinese rivals. Ironically, close to 100 Indian start-ups have raised money from Chinese investors. At about $4.6 billion in 2019, Chinese investment in Indian start-ups has grown nearly twelvefold from $381 million in 2016.[24] Of the thirty Indian unicorns (start-ups in India valued at over $1 billion), eighteen have taken Chinese investment.[25] Some, however, have started to get Chinese firms off their cap tables.

Several influential entrepreneurs in India joined the chorus and urged fellow Indians to hit back at China on the economic front—uninstall their apps, stop buying Chinese goods and instead choose Indian products, they extolled their followers. Naveen Tewari, the founder of InMobi, a company backed to the tune of over $200 million by Japanese investor Softbank and a few other investors, said in an interview with ET Now, 'This is historic because digital companies don't necessarily have boundaries and in India given the population and how digitally savvy the population is, it was important for India to control its own data and take care of its own security. Therefore, it's a great phenomenal move by the PM.' InMobi owns Roposo, a short video app that competes with bigger rival TikTok. Even Micromax is attempting a comeback from the dead. The company's co-founder posted a slick video in which he extolled fellow Indians to buy locally made products. '*Border par jo hua, woh theek nahi*

---

24 https://economictimes.indiatimes.com/small-biz/startups/newsbuzz/ chinese-investments-in-indian-start-ups-grow-12-times-to-usd-4-6-bn- in-2019-globaldata/articleshow/76647471.cms

25 Ibid.

hua,' (what happened at the border was not right) Sharma said in the video. In the next few days, Micromax announced a new brand of smartphones called 'in'.

While Xiaomi and other Chinese smartphone companies that together sell three out of four smartphones in the country haven't been directly affected yet, there is growing concern that if India–China relations deteriorate any further, things could go south for these companies. To pre-empt concerns in India, Manu Jain made public appearances presenting Xiaomi as 'more Indian in spirit than any other smartphone company'.[26] Jain told the *Economic Times* in an interview that the company has generated nearly 50,000 jobs in India; makes all its devices in India; sources 65 per cent of the components from India; stores all the data locally on servers in India; and has less than ten Chinese nationals working at Xiaomi India. 'Other brands have been here for 15-10 years. We've been here for six years, out of which our Make in India journey has been like four-and-a-half-year-old. And still, we are ahead of anybody else in localization. In spirit, we are more Indian than anybody else,' Jain said.[27] For good measure, Xiaomi covered up the frontage of its offline stores with posters of Make in India to prevent mobs from attacking the stores.

In hindsight, Xiaomi's efforts to build relationships with New Delhi after the 2014 fiasco seem to be paying off now, at a time when the relationship between India and China is at

---

26 https://economictimes.indiatimes.com/tech/hardware/facing-mob-mentality-on-social-media-but-indian-consumers-are-smart-xiaomis-jain/articleshow/76550783.cms?from=mdr

27 https://economictimes.indiatimes.com/tech/hardware/facing-mob-mentality-on-social-media-but-indian-consumers-are-smart-xiaomis-jain/articleshow/76550783.cms

its worst. Xiaomi continues to sell products through 10,000 retailers and online without too much trouble on account of souring India–China relations. With bilateral trade of $65 billion (April–December 2019), China is India's second-largest trading partner after the US. India imports nearly $20 billion worth of electrical machines, including smartphones and other devices, from China every year. In the absence of local manufacturing capacity, banning Chinese hardware may yet prove difficult, if not impossible.

An unlikely challenge

Another stumbling block in Xiaomi's path so far has been the outbreak of the COVID-19 pandemic in late 2019, which has forced countries across the world to go into national lockdowns and caused the global economy to come to a screeching halt. In December 2019, an acute respiratory syndrome called the coronavirus disease (COVID-19) was first identified in the Wuhan province of China. Since then, it has taken on pandemic proportions, spread like wildfire across the globe, affecting over 200 countries and territories by April 2020. The Xiaomi prospectus of 2018 had mentioned the impact a black swan event such as this could have on the company. It noted,

'Should major public health issues, including pandemics arise, we could be adversely affected by more stringent employee travel restrictions, additional limitations in freight services, governmental actions limiting the movement of products between regions, delays in production ramps of new products and disruptions in the operations of our outsourcing partners, component suppliers and ecosystem partners.'

To be sure, the prospectus usually contains many such blanket statements that even cover rare occurrences in the section where it outlines various risks. However, all these effects are now the lived reality of not just Xiaomi but companies all around the world. Speaking of Xiaomi in particular, the COVID crisis has affected its month-on-month sales. The company has even had to hike its prices for several products including the Redmi Note 8. In March 2020, *Business Today* reported Xiaomi saying,

'The extended shutdown was likely to have an impact on the supply chain, and we continue evaluating as the situation keeps evolving each day, but we are able to fulfill the demand as of now. While we are working to explore alternative supply channels for components and raw materials, the immediate impact is that the short supply might cause some negative pressure on prices of these components. This has led to the increase in the price of the product temporarily.'[28]

Xiaomi also faced a disruption in production. ' ... we experienced a temporary disruption in production in February and March 2020, due to the extended shutdown of Chinese factories. However, our production capacity has recovered to 80-90 per cent of normal levels as of the date of this announcement,' the

---

28 https://www.businesstoday.in/technology/news/coronavirus-impact-so-far-so-good-for-smartphone-industry/story/397848.html

company said in March 2020. In Mainland China, Xiaomi said that its offline sales were affected during the peak of the outbreak, but smartphone shipments rebounded quickly in March 2020. However, the company's overseas business in India is likely to be more severely affected. 'While our overseas demand will undoubtedly be affected, particularly in the second quarter of 2020, we believe the overall impact is currently manageable,' Xiaomi said. But with nationwide lockdowns in several countries, it will become increasingly difficult to organize launch events and even get the phones into people's hands.

It is true that Xiaomi's preference for online sales over its offline outlets has meant that its business has not been entirely affected, though the disruption in supply chains will definitely dent its overall sales performance. Xiaomi may yet recover from the short-term impact of the pandemic. A side effect of the COVID crisis is that China's economy slowed down in the first three months of 2020, for the first time since 1976. The International Monetary Fund (IMF) projects that China's growth will decline to 1.2 per cent in 2020 from 6.1 per cent in 2019. 'This sharply contrasts with China's growth performance during the Global Financial Crisis, which was little changed at 9.4 percent in 2009 thanks to the important fiscal stimulus of about 8 percent of GDP. We cannot expect that magnitude of stimulus this time, and China won't help Asia's growth as it did in 2009,' director of the Asia and Pacific Department at the IMF, Chang Yong Rhee, wrote. India's economy also shrunk by 7.5 per cent in the second quarter of 2020-21, after a 23.9 per cent decline in the previous quarter. It signals deeper troubles for companies as consumer spending will be hit. Xiaomi's sales depend on how long it takes for the economy to recover and consumer spending to go back to pre-COVID days. That recovery may yet be a long time from now.

Moreover, as Chinese firms, Xiaomi and others will likely find themselves in the line of attack after the outbreak of the epidemic. Many people, including former US President Donald Trump, have repeatedly called this pandemic a case of the 'Chinese virus', a racist slur that has stigmatized China once again as the land of ill-hygiene and diseases and held it solely responsible for causing a global crisis of disastrous proportions. From being called 'Chinese spies' to being identified as companies hailing from the land of the 'Chinese virus', these defamations have indeed cost Chinese firms their business and affected their overall performance. The COVID pandemic has also further escalated tensions between the US and China. Donald Trump has repeatedly alleged that China has not been transparent enough about the outbreak of the virus. Other US government officials have fanned the theory that the virus could have escaped from a lab in Wuhan. In the run up to the 2020 elections, Trump attacked China even more. In April 2020, in Xiaomi's biggest market India, the government announced a clampdown on investment from China.[29] The government said that Chinese entities and also entities from countries sharing land borders with India will have to seek prior approval from the government before making an investment. India's market watchdog, the Securities and Exchange Board of India, has also increased scrutiny of Chinese investments in

---

29 https://economictimes.indiatimes.com/news/economy/policy/india-steps-up-scrutiny-on-investment-from-china-and-its-neighbours/articleshow/75219816.cms

Indian companies.[30] Still, Xiaomi posted better-than-expected results in the first half of 2020.

The fight for privacy

There are two types of companies on the internet. Those that rely on advertising for revenue, such as Google and Facebook, and those that are against that model. The ad-dependent companies, if one was to take a strict view like acclaimed scholar Shoshana Zuboff, are part of a new economic order called surveillance capitalism. She defines surveillance capitalism as a practice that 'claims human experience as free raw material for hidden commercial practices of extraction, prediction, and sales'. Their business relies on knowing more and more about the users—the raw material. This extraction, of course, is not appreciated by proponents of privacy. However, products that promise greater privacy, such as Apple, tend to be more expensive and are usually targeted at the premium end-users. As users become more and more conscious of their privacy, advertising-led models could come under threat. The General Data Protection Regulation (GDPR), which came into effect in the European Union (EU) in May 2018, assures reasonable privacy to users. Online advertising is an area that has been deeply affected by the GDPR, which places several restrictions on companies tracking users for advertising. The law not only applies to companies in the EU but also to companies outside the EU that serve customers in the region online. It has already been used to penalize internet companies that rely on advertising as a source of revenue. In

---

30 https://www.livemint.com/market/stock-market-news/sebi-seeks-details-of-all-chinese-investments-in-stock-markets-11587021929995.html

January 2019, France fined Google ∈50 million, the biggest GDPR fine at the time of writing this book, alleging that Google was not transparent enough about collecting data; and that it was in violation of several articles such as lawfulness of processing data and principles relating to the processing of data.

And that's where the rub is for Xiaomi, which makes some of its internet services revenues from advertising and counts on advertising revenues for growth. In the fourth quarter of 2019 alone, the smartphone company made $424.5 million (RMB 3 billion) from advertising. In 2019, Xiaomi said that its revenue from internet services grew 24.4 per cent over the previous year to $2.8 billion (RMB 19.8 billion). Monthly active users of MIUI were at 343 million as of June 2020, making it a significant player in the advertising business. If things go their way, Xiaomi will have a healthy money spinner on its hands for the foreseeable future. But if the world tends towards more and more privacy, consumer sentiment and regulations may go against digital advertising, and it may become tougher for Xiaomi to sell and display advertisements. The advertising model evidently also creates a strategic rift for Xiaomi, which also aspires to sell premium phones. In the premium range, it launched a phone called Poco, led by Jai Mani, a product manager who was hired by Barra. According to a company source, one of Jai's biggest battles within Xiaomi was to avoid showing ads on the Poco phone. 'People barely tolerate ads on cheaper devices. But premium users would hate ads,' the former Xiaomi employee said. Mani, who left the company in July 2019, did not respond to a request for an interview.

Another challenge with Xiaomi's advertising model is that India, where it has its largest user base, is a very poor yet hyper-competitive digital advertising market. Of about $2.27 billion that was spent on digital advertising in 2019, the lion's share goes to the likes of Google and Facebook.[31] The rest is divided up between hundreds of players, including online video streaming companies, content creators, e-commerce companies and apps. The promised surge in digital advertising has not yet happened in India. Simple laws of demand and supply tell us that as more and more inventory is added to a market, there's less and less money to be made by sellers.

While questions remain about Xiaomi's advertising business, in the long run, its prospects as an internet company are not completely vague. Some green shoots of growth have started showing in the other businesses Xiaomi has incubated. 'Diversification of our internet services has become a key growth driver of our internet services revenue,' the company said in its filings. To that end, its internet services revenue outside of advertising and gaming grew 111.2 per cent. This means its e-commerce platform Youpin, fintech business, TV internet services and overseas internet services accounted for 43 per cent of its total internet services revenue. In the fourth quarter of 2019, revenue from online gaming grew by 44.4 per cent year-over-year to RMB 874.4 million as some of its games picked up. E-commerce, fintech and internet services like games, however, are several different battlefronts with tough incumbents such as Alibaba and WeChat.

In several stories of the Superman saga, the all-powerful Kryptonian eventually overcomes the effects of Kryptonite. But in the saga of Xiaomi and Lei, those chapters are yet to be written. What we can decidedly look forward to are several battles raging in the months and years to come.

---

31 https://assets.kpmg/content/dam/kpmg/in/pdf/2019/08/india-media-entertainment-report-2019.pdf

Index